Bernard E.

Y0-BWG-979

Studies in Christian Doctrine
Volume 2

Review and Herald Publishing Association
Washington, D.C. 20012

Editor: Thomas A. Davis
Book Design: Alan Forquer
Cover Illustration: Dennis Crews

Printed in U.S.A.

ACKNOWLEDGMENTS
Texts credited to N.I.V. are from *The Holy Bible: New International Version.* Copyright © 1978 by the New York International Bible Society. Used by permission of Zondervan Bible Publishers.

Quotations from N.E.B. are from *The New English Bible.* © The Delegates of the Oxford University Press and the Syndics of the Cambridge University Press 1961, 1970. Reprinted by permission.

Quotation from *The Jerusalem Bible,* copyright © 1966 by Darton, Longman & Todd, Ltd., and Doubleday & Co., Inc. Used by permission of the publishers.

Library of Congress Cataloging in Publication Data
Seton, Bernard E., 1913-
    These truths shall triumph.

    1. Seventh-day Adventists—Doctrinal and controversial works.
I. Title.
BX6154.S37   230'.673   81-8495
ISBN 0-8280-0099-9   AACR2

CONTENTS

IN CHRIST
WE BELIEVE

Once upon a time there were homes whose front doors would open to reveal to a visitor a legend burnt into a rectangle of wood, or embroidered in colored silk or wool on a strip of linen, or perhaps painted on framed parchment. The lovingly inscribed words were an unashamed declaration of family policy: "Christ is the Head of this house, the Unseen Guest at every meal, the Silent Listener to every conversation." The visitor was warned. He knew what to expect and by implication had at least a general idea of how he should behave.

Such times may now be far behind us, for times do change. We may no longer announce our allegiance so unashamedly; we may even conceal it behind a façade of sophistication, but surely the fact should remain the same—Christ should be the Head of our house and the Heart of our religion.

The two quarters' Sabbath school lessons entitled "This We Believe" have been prepared for those who wish to survey the principal doctrines of the Seventh-day Adventist Church from a slightly different angle than heretofore. There has been no compulsion to cover every detail, for that would lead to weighty tomes that would intimidate and be unsuitable for Sabbath school study. The aim has been, rather, to gauge the spirit of the teaching and to discover its Center, Jesus Christ the Righteous. If He is not naturally there—as opposed to artificially—we need to restudy our understanding of that particular article of faith and either discover the Lord or adjust the doctrine.

It should not be difficult to keep Jesus at the center of these studies, for He plays an obviously central role in many of them. We meet Him as the Apostle and High Priest of our profession, as the Judge, the returning King, the Re-creator, the Head of the church, the Lord to whom we witness, and the Sustainer of life that counts. But so easily is the human mind deflected from even the most distinct lines of thought that discipline is a constant necessity for those who wish to stay on course.

We also need to remind ourselves that in true religion even the highest and deepest flights of thought have practical objectives in view. The end is never thought in itself; it is the effect of that thought on the thinker—does it make me a better man or woman? Am I more Christlike because of my increased knowledge of Christ? Am I better prepared to meet Him by my studies of His life, His work, His character?

The overriding purpose in the pages that follow is to help writer and reader to see our many-splendored Lord as He is, and from seeing Him move to being more like Him. Jesus Himself has sent us His Spirit that that purpose might be fulfilled.

WE BELIEVE IN

OUR GREAT HIGH PRIEST

When the pagan population of Antioch in Syria gave the nickname Christians to those who followed Jesus of Nazareth, they little knew what a good turn they were doing the church. The name, itself a hybrid Greek and Latin designation, signified "those who follow Christ" and proved so apt as to remain the universal way of identifying Christ's disciples. In so doing it helped to ensure the Christ-centeredness of the new religion.

During the apostolic era it was natural for the person of Christ to fill the believers' spiritual horizon. The leaders of the early Christian community had personally known their Lord; from first-hand knowledge they could describe His physical appearance, His personal habits, the sound of His voice, the contents of His public speeches, the winsomeness of His private encounters, the manner in which He performed His miracles. They could review, in moving tones, the drama of His arrest, trial, and crucifixion; they could recount the postresurrection appearances and portray the muted majesty of the ascension. They could claim personal commission as His witnesses and appeal to His remembered authority for solution to the problems that troubled the early church.

But when the apostolic ranks were broken by death, the image of Christ inevitably grew weaker and the temptation to replace it with formalism and lifeless doctrine grew greater. It then became even more necessary for the church to cherish a conscious Christ-centeredness. That need was foreseen and met by the reality of the Saviour's priesthood. Those who could see their risen and ascended Lord continually ministering as their great High Priest had an ever-living center on which to focus their faith and spiritual consciousness. They were not left to their own devices: they were following and serving Him who was filling the central role in the government of the universe. "Wherefore, . . . " adjures the writer of Hebrews, "consider the Apostle and High Priest of our profession, Christ Jesus," "the author and finisher of our faith" (Heb. 3:1; 12:2).

Tabernacle and Temple

God has always wanted to live with those who were made in His own image. He revealed this in Eden by "walking in the garden in the cool of the day" (Gen. 3:8), but was soon cut off from His creatures by the intrusion of sin (cf. Isa. 59:2). Love was rebuffed, but not defeated. As He sought Adam and Eve after their fall, so He has ever been seeking His children, individually and corporately. When, after centuries of dealing with families, He used the occasion of the Exodus to create a nation upon which He could lavish His love, He announced His intent to "dwell among them" (Ex. 25:8). This should be recognized as the prime office of the sanctuary that was then constructed. It was designed to house the personal presence of the God who cannot bear to be parted from His people. We should not, however, think of the Almighty's limiting Himself to a few cubic feet of space—for "the most High dwelleth not in temples made with hands" (Acts 7:48)—but that His presence was there in the Most Holy Place and, indeed, that "the glory of the Lord filled the tabernacle" (Ex. 40:34; cf. 1 Kings 8:10 for Solomon's Temple, Haggai 2:7

for the second Temple, and Rev. 15:8 for the heavenly prototype). This gave His people a locale toward which they could direct their worship, their yearning after their Maker, their desire to find freedom from sin, and the means to attain that blessed liberty.

The Priest's Office

But a tabernacle or a temple, though housing that Divine Presence, could not guarantee the reconciliation of a rebellious people with their God. It needed a mediator who would communicate the Sovereign's pardoning love to His sinful subjects and persuade them to seek forgiveness and release from their sins. Such an intermediary was provided in the person of Aaron, his sons, and their successors in the priestly office. In the upward direction they were to "minister unto" the Lord "in the priest's office" (Ex. 28:1), rendering the homage that is always due to His holy name. At the same time it was their awesome responsibility to mediate the salvation that God offered His erring children and to present their people's repentance and sacrifices before the Most High (Heb. 5:1). This twofold ministry, from the people to God and from God to the people, was such a full-time occupation that it called for full-time assistance of Levites to care for the supporting services in and around the sanctuary.

Nonetheless, no matter how dedicated many of these priests were, they could serve only in an interim office since they themselves were sinful and in need of the same pardon that they sought for their people (chap. 9:7). The more perceptive of them, together with many of the prophets, realized the temporary nature of the office and longed for the appearance of the prototype Priest to whom their service pointed.

While there are anticipatory glimpses in the Old Testament of the great High Priest believers had to wait until after the ascension for a sunburst of revelation and realization concerning the holder of that unique office. When their straining eyes turned from the concealing cloud and fell once more on earthly scenes, they were ready to look with new eyes upon the national priestly system, to impose upon it the scattered references to Him who is "a priest for ever after the order of Melchizedek" who would "make his soul an offering for sin," and who "by his knowledge" would "justify many" and "bear their iniquities" (Ps. 110:4; Isa. 53:10, 11), and to begin to see their beloved Lord as the fulfiller of the old promises.

A Disregarded Ministry

In view of the clarity of New Testament revelation concerning our Lord's high priesthood, it is surprising that the long-established Christian churches have given so little attention to this aspect of His ministry. But the Epistle to the Hebrews prevents us from ignoring our Saviour's exalted office: "Jesus the Son of God" is the "great high priest, that is passed into the heaven," He has "an unchangeable priesthood," needing not daily "to offer up sacrifice, . . . for this he did once, when he offered up himself" (Heb. 4:14; 7:24, 27). The writer of Hebrews therefore concludes, "We have such an high priest, who is set on the right hand of the throne of the Majesty in the heavens; a minister of the sanctuary, and of the true tabernacle, which the Lord pitched and not man" (chap. 8:1, 2). In these words he confirms his earlier descriptions of Christ as "Apostle and High Priest of our profession," "called of God an high priest after the order of Melchisedec" (chaps. 3:1; 5:10), and emphasizes His divinity, His authority, and His intercessory work in the tabernacle, of which the earthly tent was only a shadow of the eternal heavenly original.

Enticing glimpses into heavenly places must not lead us to forget the reason for the Son's ministry in "the true tabernacle," which is sin—our sin and that of our fellows. At the same time we may need to remind ourselves that whatever the nature of heaven's architecture, it was primarily designed for the worship and glory of God and secondarily for the solution of sin. Our Lord's appointment was no afterthought, conjured up to meet an unexpected emergency, but was the realization of an eternal intention. Neither was it of a temporary nature, to be annulled when sin is forever destroyed. The Conqueror of sin will be the great, perfect, and ideal High Priest for ever and ever.

Like Unto His Brethren

Study of God's ways with man, especially for his salvation, continually elicits from the reverent mind an awed wonder at the complex unity of the plan for man's redemption. This wonder is displayed in subdued but convincing language in Hebrews 2:14-18, where the Creator is revealed as making His children in flesh and blood, well knowing, from times eternal, that He Himself would be so made at a given date in human history. He also chose the wages of sin—death—to be the means of destroying "him that had the power of death, that is, the devil." Who else but the Almighty would and could dare such a breathtaking strategy for liberating mankind and the universe from the slavery of sin?

Out of this bold plan came another inestimable blessing to the human race. Being "made like unto his brethren," the Son could be "a merciful and faithful high priest . . . , to make reconciliation for the sins of the people." Here is the implication that not even the Son of God could become the efficacious High Priest without undergoing incarnation and being "in all points tempted like as we are, yet without sin" (chaps. 2:18; 4:15). As Thomas Hewitt so perceptively observes: "The power of sympathy lies not in the mere capacity for feeling but in the lessons of experience for, having suffered *being tempted,* our High Priest *is able to succour them that are tempted,* Furthermore, the power of sympathy does not depend on the experience of sin, but on the experience of the strength of the temptation to sin which only the sinless can know in its full intensity."—*The Epistle to the Hebrews* (Tyndale Commentaries) p. 76.

Even a glimpse of the divine generosity inherent in this design makes our hearts swell with gratitude. Deeper insight into its glories should lead us to sing with P. P. Bliss in awed wonder, "Hallelujah! what a Saviour!"

Our Intercessor

One of the most precious products of our Lord's high priesthood is His intercessory service. "For Christ is not entered into the holy places made with hands . . . ; but into heaven itself, now to appear in the presence of God for us" (Heb. 9:24). This is the antitype of the typical high priest's annual entrance into the Most Holy Place of the tabernacle or temple, but with this significant difference—our High Priest, by virtue of His divinity and sinlessness, is not limited to a once-a-year appearance, but is continually in the presence of God from the days of His ascension. This is implied in the use of the adverb *now* ("now to appear in the presence of God for us") and is confirmed by such scriptures as Psalm 110:1; Mark 16:19; Luke 24:51; Acts 2:32-35 (consult various versions); Philemon 2:9; Colossians 3:1; and Hebrews 10:12 (see also *The Desire of Ages,* pp. 833-835). The crucified and resurrected Christ came into the Father's presence "for us," on our behalf, as our Advocate. We who have no strength or goodness, no wisdom of our own, cannot represent our own sinful selves before Him who is of too pure eyes to behold evil. We need the Sinless One to represent us before the Judge of all the earth who appointed Him for that very purpose.

How helpless, how bereft of hope, we sinners would be if Christ did not ever live to make intercession for us! How thankful we should continually be that He fulfilled the agreed plan that enables Him to serve as High Priest, "holy, blameless, pure, set apart from sinners, exalted above the heavens" (Heb. 7:26, N.I.V.), "who needeth not daily . . . to offer up sacrifice . . . : for this he did once, when he offered up himself" (verse 27). "Wherefore he is able also to save them to the uttermost that come unto him, seeing he ever liveth to make intercession for them" (verse 25). Our part is to "come unto God by him" in contrition, with true repentance, and in faith, knowing that He is ever, even now, living to make effective intercession on our behalf.

The Believer's Response

The Epistle to the Hebrews conveys a wealth of instruction about our great High Priest, but none of it is a mere impartation of knowledge; it all has the pastoral purpose of leading the needy sinner to the only One who can save him from his sin and present him faultless before the God who dwells "in the light which no man can approach unto; whom no man hath seen, nor can see" (1 Tim. 6:16). The Epistle has thoroughly explored the Son's high priestly credentials and found Him to be completely and eminently worthy of presenting contrite, believing souls for acceptance into His Father's kingdom. The writer then applies the purpose of this high priesthood to the daily lives of the Christian community, and does this at intervals throughout his letter, rather than leaving it all for a final exhortation (see chaps. 2:1-3; 3:1, 12-14; 4:1, 11-16; 6:1; 12:1, 2; etc.).

From the abundant counsel offered in the Epistle, three passages may be chosen to summarize the

implications of the Saviour's priesthood for the individual believer. The first concerns the believer's approach
to God (Heb. 4:16). The Christian, though a sinner—
indeed because he is sinful—is invited, even urged, to
approach "the throne of grace," that is, the throne where
grace is dispensed (which can only be the throne where
the God of all grace reigns). This should be done
"boldly," or with confidence, for there we shall obtain
mercy, there we shall find the Giver of the grace that will
help us in all times of need. This will not be a one-time
appearance for any of us. Many will be our times of
need. We are therefore being exhorted to keep on
coming to God, through the mediation of our divine
High Priest.

Approaching God With Confidence

The second choice is found in chapter 10:19-25
where the brethren—that is, the believers—are
reminded of the New Testament privilege of direct
access into the holy places (plural) or the entire
sanctuary, God's dwelling place, by virtue of Christ's
sacrificed blood and His priesthood. This redemptive
ministry makes it possible for us to approach God
confidently ("in full assurance of faith"), with purified
hearts and cleansed bodies. We should, therefore,
maintain an unwavering faith and so practice our
religion that we encourage others also to be steadfast
unto the day of Christ's appearing.

The third and final exhortation is the regal bene-
diction written in chapter 13:20, 21. In majestic
sublimity the writer prays, amid the turmoils of his
day, that God, the Author of peace and the Resurrector
of "our Lord Jesus, that great shepherd of the sheep,"
will perfect his readers in the doing of God's will.
This, he recognizes, will be accomplished only
through the blood of the everlasting covenant, which
is both shed and administered by the High Priest

Himself, that is, Jesus Christ. The answer to this prayer should be the bringing of eternal glory either to the God of peace or to Jesus Christ, or, in reality, to both these members of the Godhead. This should be the fruitage of belief in the Apostle and High Priest of our profession, Christ Jesus.

WE BELIEVE IN

JUDGMENT, THE JUDGE, AND THE JUDGED

No right-thinking person denies the doctrine of accountability. It is indeed difficult to formulate any philosophy of life without subscription to the ethic of responsibility for our words and actions. The Christian goes further and on Biblical authority also includes responsibility for thoughts. It should then come as no surprise to find that the prospect of judgment looms large on the Biblical landscape.

The reality of judgment was built into the creation of all moral beings, principalities, powers, and angels, as well as men and women. The Creator made all His creatures perfect, but He did not want automatons who would do His will mechanically. He designed free moral agents who would do right from choice, though the provision of free will made wrongdoing possible. Their freedom, therefore, carried with it moral responsibility for both right- and wrongdoing. This leads to accountability and judgment, with the Creator becoming the Judge.

From Heaven's viewpoint judgment is instantaneous, in that there is no need for the All-wise, the All-knowing, to hesitate on pronouncement of right and wrong, though execution of sentence may not take place for many a year. But all observers are not endowed with divine understanding, and the wrongdoer may not always be convinced of his error. For all such, some form of judicial procedure is necessary that right judgment may be discerned and justice seen to have been done. This calls for some form of reckoning day, a time when all moral beings will hear divine judgment pronounced and be persuaded that it is undeniably just.

To those who know their God none of the above causes lasting personal concern, for they know that He does all things well, and they trust His judgments. At the same time, the Christian is judgment-conscious, aware that he must appear before the judgment seat and give account for all that he has done. To that knowledge he adds a saving assurance—the promise of an Advocate, Jesus Christ the Righteous, who is the propitiation for his confessed sins and who is well able to represent him before the righteous Judge. Nevertheless, awareness of judgment serves to guide the Christian in present conduct and to prepare him for Christ's public and decisive acknowledgment of being his personal Saviour.

In subscribing to such concepts we should be careful to avoid a rigid application of the human judicial process to the heavenly procedures, "for my thoughts are not your thoughts, neither are your ways my ways, saith the Lord" (Isa. 55:8). When we have sought to determine the time and manner of judgment, our principal thoughts should still center on Christ our Judge, our Advocate, our merciful and faithful High Priest, who makes reconciliation for the sins of us, His people (Heb. 2:17).

Subject to Judgment

It is surely noteworthy that the first recorded words that the Creator God addressed to the newly formed Adam and Eve outlined their initial responsibilities. They were to be fruitful, having children, populating the unspoiled globe on which their Maker had placed them. They were to establish control over the earth and its animal inhabitants, guiding them into legitimate service for mankind (Gen. 1:28). From the parallel Creation account preserved in Genesis, chapter 2, we learn that "the Lord God took the man, and put him in the garden of Eden to dress it and to keep it. And the Lord God commanded the man, saying, of every tree of the garden thou mayest freely eat: but of the tree of the knowledge of good and evil, thou shalt not eat of it" (verses 15-17). In so speaking, the Lord placed responsibility upon the perfect pair and made them accountable for their conduct and management of the new creation. In other words, they were subject to judgment.

The brief record, covering we know not how many years, shows that both husband and wife were aware of God's instructions (see Gen. 3:1-3) and knew that disobedience would eventually bring death. Their experience of life had been too short for them to learn all of its lessons and secrets, but their high level of unweakened intelligence convinced them of the justice of the decree, and they recognized that the still-unknown tragedy of death would be the natural outcome of transgression, the fruitage of, rather than the punishment for, sin. In this they anticipated the final verdict that will acknowledge that God's judgments, far from being arbitrary or vengeful, embody the perfect laws around which the universe functions.

God and Judgment

Since, for weal or woe, everything we do is subject to judgment, it behooves us to care well for our deeds, our words, and our thoughts. In the Old Testament this is recommended by the preacher when he writes, "Fear God and keep his commandments: for this is the whole duty of man. For God shall bring every work into judgment, with every secret thing, whether it be good, or whether it be evil" (Eccl. 12:13, 14). Those verses bear thoughtful consideration. "Fear" is not a craven response to a tyrant but a wholesome loving respect for the Almighty (cf. Ps. 19:9). "His commandments" are not to be limited to the Decalogue, but should include all the wise counsel He gives us in addition to the ten precepts (study Ps. 19:7-11 with that interpretation in mind). The fact that "God shall bring every work into judgment, . . . whether it be evil" shows that our whole conduct is surveyed, debit and credit, so a balanced assessment is made; while the inclusion of "every secret thing" indicates examination of the thoughts and intents of the heart.

This prospect is confirmed by none other than the Lord Jesus as He reasoned with critical Pharisees: "I say unto you, That every idle word that men shall speak, they shall give account thereof in the day of judgment" (Matt. 12:36). This need not paint a picture of petty bookkeeping, for general conduct will often eliminate the need for detailed examination, but the record is there for reference, for praise or blame, if the need for either should arise. Those who know God best will not be surprised by either the preacher's or Christ's declaration, for they will remember the Creator's incalculable capacity for breadth and minuteness of knowledge, believing Him to be "he which searcheth the reins and hearts" (Rev. 2:23), "a discerner of the thoughts and intents of the heart" (Heb. 4:12). They will realize that the Omniscient One does not need a judgment for His own information; any assize that is held is for the defendant's and the public's benefit.

The character of that all wise, all just Judge is our best assurance of the rectitude of the judgment; there is no bias in its deliberations. "All his commandments are sure." They are "done in truth and uprightness" (Ps. 111:7, 8). We may therefore have complete confidence, both for ourselves and for others, in His verdict. Indeed, we may sing with the psalmist: "Let the hills be joyful together before the Lord; for he cometh to judge the earth: with righteousness shall he judge the world, and the people with equity" (Ps. 98:8, 9).

Judgment on Earth

After making historical allowance for difference in time and place, much can be learned for our own enlightenment from the Hebrew economy established by Moses under divine authority. In the Pentateuch—especially in the book of Leviticus, where the tabernacle services are described—there is careful instruction for dealing with human frailties that lead to petty and major crimes and unneighborly acts. It is significant that the general purpose is toward forgiveness rather than to punishment, toward rehabilitation of the delinquent rather than his condemnation, while not condoning his sin or allowing him to escape from making suitable restitution.

When prescribed, even costly, rituals are observed and contrition is expressed in suitable words and deeds according to priestly judgment, pardon is obtained and right relationships toward neighbors, the nation, and to God are reestablished. In many instances the priest served as judge and mediator, representing the sinner before the presence of the Lord in the sanctuary (Lev. 6:6, 7, and parallels).

Daily performance of such service relieved the transgressor of the immediate burden of delinquency, but figuratively brought into the tabernacle, and later the Temple, an accumulation of guilt that called for a yearly atonement that would clear the records and give the individual and the nation a clean beginning for a new year. The annual Day of Atonement met that need through its ritual of cleansing and pardon (Lev. 16).

In Hebrews 9:22-26 the New Testament relates the Old Testament ritual to the post-ascension ministry of Christ in the heavenly temple where He entered into the holy places that had been typified by the earthly sanctuary, there "to appear in the presence of God for us

. . . to put away sin by the sacrifice of himself." There lies the hope of pardon for our sin.

Judgment in Heaven

One of Seventh-day Adventism's unique contributions to the interpretation of Biblical prophetic literature lies in its exposition of Daniel 8:14. Relating the words, "Unto two thousand and three hundred days; then shall the sanctuary be cleansed" to the later prophecy recorded in Daniel 9:24-27, it teaches that the 2300 prophetic days represent literal years, with 457 B.C. marking the commencement and A.D. 1844 the terminal date for that long time period. The term "cleansing of the sanctuary" is applied to the temple of God in heaven, where the Saviour has been interceding on our behalf since He ascended to the Father, and to an antitypical day of atonement for the cleansing of the sanctuary by an act of judgment based on the Son's shed blood, which will clear the records of all who have trusted in Christ for their salvation.

To that picture there should be added the vivid scene portrayed by Daniel's earlier vision (chap. 7:9, 10), where "the judgment was set, and the books were opened" before the majestic Ancient of days, and where "one like a son [rather than "the Son"] of man" came "with the clouds of heaven" (verse 13, R.S.V.). From this we may discern the judgment in heaven merging into the Second Advent.

There is much to commend such an interpretation. It holds fast to the portrayal of the resurrected Jesus as our great High Priest serving on His people's behalf in the heavenly sanctuary, where they cannot yet enter. It provides heavenly meaning to the typical daily priestly ministry on the one hand and to the annual Day of Atonement on the other. It also closely relates to the last days, seeing antitypical cleansing in heaven as the culmination of redemptive activity immediately prior to the Second Coming of our Lord.

There are also dangers to be avoided, one of the least of which may be our tendency to interpret the eternal too literally in terms of the temporal illustration. We may need to be less rigid in some of our applications and to make more room for the vastness and majesty of the unseen, not yielding to the temptation to create a restricted image from the types that God gave.

New Testament and Judgment

Under the impetus of Christ's personal teaching and the continuing instruction of the Holy Spirit, the early Christians became keenly aware of coming judgment and shared their knowledge and convictions with both Jews and pagans. Early in His ministry their Master had broached the subject and fixed firm parameters that defined the field for His followers. After healing the cripple at Bethesda the Lord had to defend Himself against skeptical Jews who disputed His claims to divinity. In reply He declared that the Father had "committed all judgment unto the Son" and had "given him authority to execute judgment," plainly assuming responsibility for both the forensic and the executive aspects of judgment. There could certainly be no better hands than His—nail-pierced—into which to fall for judgment. That Judge wants to save His creatures: He died for that very purpose; the Father delegated life-giving powers to Him that He might give life to all who believe on Him and the Father (see John 5:22-29).

The lesson was not lost on the disciples and later leaders. As Peter outlined the gospel to Cornelius and his household in Caesarea, he faithfully presented his risen Lord as "Judge of quick and dead" (Acts 10:40-42), while Paul, using similar words, urged his Athenian audience to repent in view of the coming judgment. God "hath appointed a day," declared the apostle, when He will righteously "judge the world . . . by that man whom he hath ordained," that is, by the resurrected Jesus (chap. 17:30, 31).

The Epistle to the Hebrews, exploring the office and work of the heavenly High Priest, also finds judgment included in the divine program. After establishing the once-for-all nature of Christ's sacrifice and explaining that He thereby "put away," or annulled, or destroyed, the power of sin (Heb. 9:25, 26), Paul reminds his readers that all humans die and are then, in a final sense, subject to judgment (verse 27). To "them that look for him [Jesus]" that prospect need cause no fear, for to them He will "appear the second time" apart from sin to effect their salvation (verse 28).

Preparation for Judgment

As Biblical teaching on judgment is examined it becomes clear that the outcome of any investigation held depends on two factors: (1) the quality of life that has been lived by the person who is being judged and (2) the relation of that individual to the Judge, who is also Advocate and Saviour. Each of the two is necessary, and neither can be separated from the other in the context of judgment. If one lives an apparently exemplary life but rejects the Redeemer's saving role in his religious experience, he will stand defenseless in the judgment day because he has not recognized or acknowledged that "there is none righteous, no, not one" (Rom. 3:10), and that he, with all other members of the human race, needs to be covered with the righteousness of Christ. If, on the other hand, he lives a careless and sinful life and presumes to depend on Christ's pleading his cause, a shock awaits him, for the Lord will say, "I never knew you: depart from me" (Matt. 7:23).

The right preparation for judgment consists in admission with all saints that we are "carnal, sold under sin," and that in us dwells no good thing (Rom. 7:14-18). When we do this, confessing our sinfulness, Jesus "is faithful and just to forgive us our sins, and [no less important] to cleanse us from all unrighteousness" (1 John 1:9). He will then be able and willing to serve as our Advocate with the Father (chap. 2:1), and we shall be flawlessly represented before the tribunal by Him "which taketh away the sin of the world" (John 1:29).

We may study the certainty of judgment, we may learn all that the Scriptures teach concerning the time of the judgment, we may be well versed in the judicial procedures, we may visualize the awe-inspiring splendors of the judgment scene, but the one indispensable essential may still be lacking—union with Christ. "If a man abide not in me," says the Saviour, "he is cast forth as a branch . . . ; and men gather them, and cast them into the fire, and they are burned" (chap. 15:6). Therefore, pleads the Beloved Disciple, "Little children, abide in him; that, when he shall appear, we may have confidence, and not be ashamed before him at his coming" (1 John 2:28)—nor at His judgment seat!

WE
BELIEVE
IN

RECALL TO WORSHIP

What shame on the human race that it should ever need a recall to worship! It should be so keenly aware of God's majesty, His holiness, His power, His goodness, His care, His unchanging love, that praise and adoration should instinctively flow from hearts, lips, and lives.

With regret we must confess that ours is not a worshipful age. We are furnished with so many technical marvels that our sense of wonder is blunted, and we have lost much of our awareness of the numinous, that consciousness of the spiritual realities that transcends the humdrum rhythm of the earthly. But this is no valid reason for failing to acknowledge the greatness of our Creator, for failing to "give unto the Lord the glory due unto his name." It might, indeed, be persuasively argued that this lack of praise makes it even more imperative for us to worship the Lord.

We shall need some help in this area, for our devotional capacities at their best are weak. We might well employ Henry Lyte's words that conclude a hymn that should never be omitted from any God-respecting hymnbook:

> "Angels, help us to adore Him—
> Ye behold Him face to face;
> Sun and moon, bow down before Him;
> Dwellers all in time and space,
> Praise Him! praise Him! praise Him! praise Him!

Praise with us the God of grace!''

And that, believe it or not, is apropos of the judgment and belief in the judgment-hour message that holds such a central place in Adventist theology. The core of the message, of course, is far older than the historical setting in which the message is set. It is older than the hills, for "Before the hills in order stood, Or earth received her frame, From everlasting Thou art God, To endless years the same." But the subject for study in this chapter strikes the same theme, in a modern setting, by considering the call to "fear God, and give glory to him; . . . worship him that made heaven, and earth, and the sea, and the fountains of waters" (Rev. 14:7). This, according to the Revelator, is a prime part of "the everlasting gospel" (verse 6).

The Globe and the Gospel

For a full appreciation of the three messages prophetically foretold in Revelation 14:6-12 an expository study of their preceding and succeeding contexts is ideally called for, but since there is not space here for such study, we must be content with a summary statement. The vision of three angels flying in the midst of heaven is clearly given in a last-day setting—the drama depicted in chapter 13 and the eschatological coming of Him who is "like a son of man" described in chapter 14:14 (N.I.V.) point to the end of time. This gives a unique urgency to the global preaching of an (rather than "the") everlasting gospel; it might be called a last chance for the proclamation and acceptance of the eternal Good News that is to be shared with "every nation, kindred, and tongue, and people" (verse 6), before the end of human history comes.

The heart of the threefold message should not be lost in an anatomical study of the bare bones of the proclamation. It is the gospel that is to be preached. And why? Because it has been diluted, distorted, and sometimes lost since the apostolic days when it was presented in its New Testament purity. Now, before its raison d'être loses immediacy, it needs to be preached in its pristine power so that all men, women, and children may have the opportunity of accepting salvation from sin and enjoying eternal life. Each phase of the total message must surely confront its hearers with the Pentecostal gospel call—"Repent, then, and turn to God, so that your sins may be wiped out, that times of refreshing may come from the Lord, and that he may send the Christ, who has been appointed for you—even Jesus" (Acts 3:19, 20, N.I.V.). This, the heart, can then beat strongly amid the bones and flesh of the pertinent chronological frame provided by each angel's message.

Further emphasis must be given to the global extent of the prophesied preaching. In harmony with the Saviour's own instruction, "this gospel of the kingdom shall be preached in all the world for a witness unto all nations" (Matt. 24:14), and this can never be a one-time thing; it must be a continuous fulfillment of the commission, addressed not merely to a geographical or political territory but to individual human beings, to people, to "them that dwell on the earth." No mere tokenism will suffice here. All God's children need the opportunity to hear and the freedom to accept the gospel. A little arithmetic shows us that very little of the world's population has been touched and that much— very much—remains to be done!

Call to Worship

What does the gospel-giving angel proclaim to earth's inhabitants? "Fear God, and give glory to him" (Rev. 14:7). The need for the gospel resides in the historical fact that men, in every age, have failed to fear God and consequently have felt free to follow their own inclinations. The verb *fear* in this context does not imply being afraid of the Almighty, but refers to having a

wholesome respect for, a reverence for, God, a recognition of His might and majesty, His holiness, His love,
His totally incomparable character. When we and others
truly see that character, especially as it is revealed in the
Person of His Son, there will be born in us deep
reverence for and adoration of our Maker that will show
itself in respect, obedience, service, and the desire to
bring Him glory by the way we live. A natural
expression of these sentiments is worship, both private
and public, as the second half of the first message makes
clear. At this juncture, the emphasis is on godly fear,
such as is encouraged in the Psalms and Proverbs,
where the Hebrew word (verb, *yârê'*; noun, *yiŕâh*)
implies reverence rather than the state of being afraid
(e.g., Ps. 5:7; 19:9; 33:8; 34:9; 72:5; 86:11; Prov. 1:7; 8:13;
14:26; 19:23; etc.).

In the Old Testament the Hebrew word that denotes
"glory" *(kâbôd)* most frequently refers to the honor and
glory of God; the same is true for the Greek word *dŏxa* in
the New Testament. In both cases the essential reference
is to the Lord's character, which reveals its inconceivable purity in an effulgence, "the light which no man
can approach unto," the "consuming fire" before which
no man stands (1 Tim. 6:16; Heb. 12:29). A glimpse of
this glory induces in man a reverence that leads him to
give glory or honor to the altogether Holy One.

The immediate reason given for this call to glorify
God is the arrival of "the hour of his judgment." As the
SDA Bible Commentary observes (comment on Rev.
14:7), this is "not a literal hour" but "the general time
when the judgment will take place. . . . Seventh-day
Adventist expositors understand the judgment here
mentioned as that which began in 1844, represented in
type by the cleansing of the earthly sanctuary (see on
Dan. 8:14). That the reference here is not to the
executive judgment at the coming of Christ when all
receive their rewards, is seen by the fact that the

messages of the three angels (Rev. 14:6-12) precede the second coming of Christ (v. 14). Furthermore, the message concerning the judgment is accompanied by an appeal and a warning that reveal that the day of salvation has not passed."

Worship the Creator

In spite of its importance the announcement of the judgment hour is not the message of the first angel; it is rather the reason for that message. The message itself is twofold—"Fear God, and give glory to him," and "worship him that made heaven, and earth." The two sections are inextricably related and are indeed two parts of one whole. The first has been considered in the preceding section; the second gives a similar message with concentration on God's creatorship as a principal reason for our worship. This was most timely for the midnineteenth century, when the doctrine of fiat creation was being so fiercely assailed by the fast-developing theory of evolution, with Charles Darwin's *On the Origin of Species* appearing in 1859.

The antidote to the evolutionist's specious teachings lies in a well-reasoned exposition of the Biblical doctrine of creation and in the practice of its precepts in an intelligent, sincere, and consistent worship of the Creator. Hence the apocalyptic emphasis on godly fear, the giving of glory, and on worship. In the context of Creation this must undeniably include the worship of the Creator on the day He "ended his work which he had made," when He rested and "blessed the seventh day, and sanctified it," and later bade His people to "remember the sabbath day, to keep it holy" (Gen. 2:2, 3; Ex. 20:8). Faithful observance of the seventh-day Sabbath is a bulwark against destructive skepticism and bears a quiet, consistent, impressive witness to the observer's Biblical faith. But it needs to guard against deadening formalism and forgetfulness of the God-given purpose enshrined in Sabbathkeeping—the worship of the Lord of the Sabbath and the spiritual, social, and physical refreshment of the Sabbathkeeper. True remembrance of the sanctity of the seventh day enables the Christian to fulfill the behests of the first angel.

Come Out of Babylon

While the first angel's message was being preached in the 1840s the second angel's voice was also heard in the cry, "Babylon is fallen, is fallen, that great city, because she made all nations drink of the wine of the wrath of her fornication" (Rev. 14:8). When this was linked with the messages contained in Revelation 18:1-4, both were interpreted as calls for Bible-believing Christians to come out of churches that had abandoned their pristine adherence to God's Word and were teaching such un-Biblical doctrines as Sunday sacredness, the natural immortality of the soul, and an illicit union between church and state. While the message was preached by Millerites as they sought to prepare a people for Christ's return in 1844, the substance of the cry has continuing significance for all God's children, for they should ever be truth seekers, ready to return to pure New Testament theology.

The sounding of the call is evidence that many of God's people are still in popular churches that have departed from gospel standards. The continuance of the invitation for the sincere to come out of Babylon indicates that many will respond, and it is the duty of all who hold to the faith once delivered to the saints to encourage all such to answer the call, to come out, and to join those who are preparing for our Lord's return. This requires an active evangelism among all peoples that they may be instructed in scriptural teaching and led to abandon error and embrace truth. As in the parable, so in real life—the King's servants must go into the highways and hedges of our world and compel men

and women to come in to the marriage supper of the
King's Son. Compulsion must come from a twofold
power—that of truth and love—and, if there be any
difference in virtue between the two, the greater of these
is love. As Edwin Markham wrote in his poem,
"Outwitted":

> "He drew a circle that shut me out—
> Heretic, rebel, a thing to flout.
> But Love and I had the wit to win:
> We drew a circle that took him in!"

Beware of Apostasy

The third message, no less than the first and second,
cannot be understood apart from the wider background
of the neighboring chapters in the Apocalypse, particu-
lary the twelfth, thirteenth, seventeenth, and eighteenth. With their aid we see the supreme apostate
power, designated Bablyon, fighting against God and
trying to usurp authority that belongs to Him alone. In
chapter twelve we see the dragon, Satan, warring
against the church with such success that the faithful
are reduced to a remnant who become the object of his
concentrated hatred (verses 13-17). In chapter thirteen,
in a close-up of the final phases of the persecution, the
devil is shown working through similar but later
agencies to crush all who reject his mark or sign of
allegiance (verses 15-17).

God's response to this challenge comes in the third
angel's message. On the surface the two decrees look
similar, for both threaten death for noncompliance, the
one for refusal to accept false religion, the other for
rendering the worship demanded. One of the differ-
ences lies in the results, for death from the first will be
only temporary, while death from the second cause will
be eternal.

Adventists perceive in the somewhat mysterious

"mark of the beast" (chaps. 13:16-18; 14:9, 11) attempts by apostate ecclesiastical powers, allied with civil authorities, to enforce Sunday observance on large sections of our world's population, with obedience to divine law being the deeper issue and acceptance or rejection of the lordship of Christ and God being the final question that faces every responsible being. Under such circumstances the question of seventh-day Sabbathkeeping will play a critical role by revealing whether we obey God or man.

The fearful judgment pronounced upon those who choose to obey God's adversaries in lieu of being loyal to the Lord can be rightly evaluated, and then no more than dimly, only by recalling the millenniums of patience shown by the Creator in dealing with His recalcitrant creatures and by looking upon His crucified Son, who died to save men from their waywardness and its destructive results.

Neither the doctine of eternal torment nor that of eternal death should be decided on the basis of these few verses (9-11), for they were not recorded for that purpose. They are God's answer to the edicts issued by evil agents, the dragon and his minions (chap. 13:15-18), and reflect divine abhorrence of the arrogant claims made against the Lord and His faithful followers. Their severity underlines the importance of the issue at stake, namely, loyalty to God set against obedience to the apostate power.

True Worshipers

The apocalyptic recall to true worship concludes on a worshipful note in Revelation 14:12. Here, in contrast to those who worship the beast and his image, we meet those who display three of the qualities that are essential to right worship—patient saintliness, obedience, and the faith of Christ. These qualities are part of the hallmark that attests the genuineness of those who profess Christianity.

Saints have always needed patience in pursuit of their goal of Christlikeness. "In the world ye shall have tribulation," promised the Master (John 16:33) in a forecast that has been amply fulfilled during the intervening nineteen centuries. Now, near the close of time, when the devil "knoweth that he hath but a short time" and consequently has more than usual wrath against those who are loyal to God, that tribulation will be intensified (Rev. 12:12). Those who have the spiritual temerity to defy the ungodly powers can expect, though they should not seek, persecution. They will need all the fortitude with which Heaven can equip them. Still more, and primarily, they will need the saintly character that will qualify them for the record, "here is the patience of the saints." Neither they nor we shall need to show much concern about tribulation unless they and we possess the holy characters that arouse the devil's wrath! When we qualify for his attentions we shall receive them, and we will also be granted strength to bear them.

The second notable characteristic of those who emerge from last-day trials is that of obedience: they keep the commandments of God; they observe the precepts of the Decalogue in spirit as well as letter and do this from love to God and not from compulsion. But they respect more than the Ten Commandments. They do all of God's biddings, delighting to do His will, seeking to fulfill His wise, good, pleasure, and knowing that such a course produces true happiness for themselves, their families, their friends, and those who come within their orbit. In short, they bring their entire lives into obedience to the divine will.

These unnamed God-fearers also "keep . . . the faith of Jesus." The phrase is open to several commendable interpretations, of which there are almost as many as there are translations. Most standard versions in

European tongues refer to the faith which Jesus Himself had, implying that this is the class of faith possessed by those who have refused to bow down to apostate religion. Many modern English language translations, however, are more subjective, speaking of "faith in Jesus." A solution to the dilemma, if it be such, is to accept both interpretations, knowing that one cannot have the faith *of* Jesus without having faith *in* Jesus and vice versa. The spiritual imperative lies not in the translation but in the possession of the same spirit that actuated the Master and gave Him His fortitude, His perfect obedience to His Father's will, and His faith to be true even unto death. Those who emulate their Lord in these ways will be among those who worship the Father in spirit and in truth. "The Father," be it remembered, "seeketh such to worship him," especially in these last days.

WE
BELIEVE
IN

THE COMING OF THE KING

The coming of the King is an indispensable feature in the landscape of terrestial and celestial history. Without it not only would there be an empty space on the vast canvas of events but the whole composition of the picture would be ruined, the carefully placed lines would lead to a gaping hole, the placement of light and shade, color, figures, earth and sea and sky, would be meaningless. In less pictorial and starker terms the first advent of Jesus would have raised hopes that will never be fulfilled, there would be no triumph over sin, and God would not be vindicated.

Praise be! We are not left to face that gloomy prospect. The Second Advent is as certain as the realities of Creation, the Incarnation, and the sinless life and vicarious death of our Lord. In the complex jigsaw puzzle that we call history, it is one of the few remaining pieces that are waiting to fall into place. A few major events in each decade can be seen as smaller pieces that gradually add to the picture until only one more piece will be needed to complete the scene—the appearance of Christ Himself.

Movement in the Biblical view of history is inexorably toward the Second Coming. Its coming can be discerned in Genesis, it intermittently appears in the remainder of the Old Testament, comes into its own in the New, and shines in all its radiance in the Apocalypse.

When Daniel receives a God's-eye view of sections of imperial history, he sees it culminating in the establishment of the kingdom of God. Babylon, Medo-Persia, Greece, and Rome and its successors, all of intense importance to those who were living under their sway, sink into insignificance before the indestructible kingdom that will be set up by the God of heaven (Dan. 2:44). Each kingdom needs a king, and the eternal one is no exception—it needs and receives an eternal King, none other than the Son of Man, to whom is given "dominion, and glory, and a kingdom, that all people, nations, and languages, should serve him: his kingdom is an everlasting dominion, which shall not pass away" (chap. 7:14). It is the Second Coming that inaugurates this kingdom before the eyes of a watching universe, and it is that coming which now claims our attention.

There are many facets to the Incarnation, each of which has superlative value in specific sections of our lives. But the supreme purpose, clearly declared at the time of the annunciation, was the restoration of the kingdom that had been disrupted by the intrusion of sin into Eden. As Gabriel announced to Mary: "The Lord God shall give unto him [Jesus] the throne of his father David: . . . and of his kingdom there shall be no end" (Luke 1:32, 33). Until that intention is fulfilled, God cannot be King over the whole earth, and the problem of sin remains. When "Jesus shall reign where'er the sun Does his successive journeys run," then "a King shall reign and prosper, and shall execute judgment and justice in the earth" (Jer. 23:5), then "shall the righteous flourish"; "and men shall be blessed in him" (Ps. 72:7, 17).

But first the kingdom had to be wrested from the evil one. This was done through the sinless life, substitutionary death, and triumphant resurrection of the Son. In confident anticipation of the victory He could say to His Father, "I have finished the work which thou gavest me to do," and a few hours later could cry from the cross, "It is finished" (John 17:4; 19:30). But the struggle was not over until He walked from the tomb, thereby defeating "him that had the power of death" (Heb. 2:14). Even then much remained to be done prior to His ascension, particularly the launching of the church on its evangelistic career, that whosoever will might find salvation and be prepared for citizenship in the everlasting kingdom. When the church's mission is completed, there will be no reason for the Lord to delay His return. He will be free to descend from heaven with the shout that will raise the dead and unite them with the living, that all might together be ever with their Lord (1 Thess. 4:16, 17). Eternal life in the eternal kingdom will then in reality have begun.

Yet Christ's restorative work is not complete, for the earth lies desolate, and the unrepentant and their leader still have not made their last desperate attempt to overthrow God's government. The final outcome, however, is assured by virtue of the Second Coming. Its power and its glory will convince even the most skeptical that the meek will inherit the earth.

Satisfaction Assured

While we mortals do not know how the eternal mind works, enough is said in Scripture to reveal that Christ's foreknowledge did not prevent His needing reassurance during His long struggle against evil in all its horrible forms. The assurance came from communion with His Father, from celestial encouragement, from knowledge of the plans laid before the foundation of the world, and from His knowledge of and implicit trust in all revealed in the Old Testament.

Isaiah 53 must surely have been one of His favorite passages! Prophecy of His sufferings would not deter Him—He had long, long before agreed to be the slain Lamb (2 Tim. 1:9; Titus 1:2, 3; 1 Peter 1:20; Rev. 13:8),

His divine foreknowledge prepared Him for the treatment He would receive from human hands, and He "stedfastly set his face to go to Jerusalem" (Luke 9:51), there to endure the worst that men could do to Him and there also to "be received up" into the glory He had left for Bethlehem and beyond.

The Gospels also reveal that Jesus looked beyond the immediate glory that would come to Him at the ascension to the majesty that would return to Him when His kingdom would be fully restored and peopled by those whom He had saved from sin and prepared for eternity. This certainty peeps through many of the revelations given to disciples and close friends (John 1:51; 11:25; 14:1-3; Matt. 16:27; 19:28; 24:14, 29-31; 25:31-34), as well as through more public utterances (John 5:24-29; 6:40; Matt. 26:64). No matter how dark were the days on earth, the Son of God could see "the glory that should follow" (1 Peter 1:11). It was this confidence that enabled Him to "see of the travail of his soul" and to "be satisfied" (Isa. 53:11).

The total witness of Scripture leaves no room for doubt about the final outcome of the Godhead's agelong planning for the resolution of the sin question. The eye of Deity, untroubled by distance in space or time—for whom, indeed, there is neither space nor time—sees the triumph as clearly as the travail. Through foresights granted to Daniel we may share in that certainty and see the Son of man being given "dominion, and glory, and a kingdom, . . . which shall not pass away, and . . . which shall not be destroyed" (see Dan. 7:14).

Contemplation of our Lord's long-range thinking and vision raises the question "Will He be satisfied with me?" Will He see of the long, long travail of His soul on my behalf and feel that it has been well worthwhile?

Knowledge such as Jesus possessed, even in His humanity, could not remain refrigerated in His own bosom. His chosen friends, on whose shoulders would rest the weight of responsibility for steering the church through the troubled seas of first-century history, needed more than a glimpse of the eternal kingdom that their Master knew so well from eternity past and that He could see so clearly in the future, which is His eternal present. He took care, therefore, to share with them all that their humanity could bear. He told them about His Father's house, where there is room for all who want to live with Him. One reason for His departure, He explained, was "to prepare a place" for them and those who would also believe in Him (John 14:1-3). From time to time, both before and after their Lord's parting instruction, they caught gleams of the glory to which he was returning. In their moments of deepest perception they penetrated beyond the Palestinian garb and saw the Son of God in their Companion, and the revelation invigorated their witness from the slopes of Olivet, through Pentecost, to their own martyrdom.

"If I go and prepare a place for you, I will come again," said the Master just prior to His passion. They saw Him go. "He was taken up; and a cloud received him out of their sight." While they strained to keep their departing Lord in view, even after the cloud had hidden Him from their eyes, they heard words that affirmed what Christ Himself had told them: "This same Jesus . . . shall so come in like manner as ye have seen him go into heaven" (Acts 1:9-11). This assurance they joined with the information the Master had previously given them (see Matt. 24:29-31 and parallels), with it went confidently back to Jerusalem, and began to share their knowledge and convictions with any who would listen —and thousands proved themselves willing.

Signs of Return—I

It is not mere curiosity nor desire to possess forbidden knowledge that prompts the oft-repeated question, "What shall be the sign of thy coming, and of the end of the world?'' There is a need to know the answer to the double inquiry. The two events are too important for casual treatment. The fate of billions upon billions of human beings, and of the universe itself, depends on the response.

We know that Jesus understood the importance of His friends' question, for most of the information they obtained and later used came from His lips. We may be no less sure that any vagueness in His replies came not from lack of knowledge but from His understanding of the questioners' capacities and of the immensity of the topic. But we need to distinguish between His forecasts concerning the A.D. 70 destruction of Jerusalem and the far more distant signs proclaiming His own return and the end of the world. Such distinctions are not easy to make and are not always necessary, for some of the signs apply to both events, as, for example, the wars and rumors of wars, the famines, pestilences, and earthquakes, which have also preceded and accompanied other world cataclysms. Our concentration needs to be upon the more particular signs given by the Saviour.

For A.D. 70 the most specific warnings relate to Daniel's prophecies and the need for flight from the doomed Jewish capital (Matt. 24:15-20). These counsels must refer to the Roman siege of Jerusalem, for flight (verses 16-20) would be of no avail at the end of the world.

But our concern must needs be focused upon far greater events associated with the Second Coming and the end of human mismanagement of the world. These may be seen foreshadowed in verses 21 to 28 of Matthew 24, where there are unmistakable references to last-day happenings. The great tribulation (verses 21, 22) and anticipation of Christ's return (verses 23-28) belong in the doctrine of last things and indicate the time on which Christ's mind was set as He shared His knowledge with the twelve.

Signs of Return—II

The clearest references to the Second Advent are broached halfway through our Lord's prophecy. As the end draws near it becomes increasingly important for specific information to be gained concerning the time and manner of His appearing. He therefore confirms earlier predictions that speak of the darkening of sun and moon, the falling of stars, and the shaking of the "powers of the heavens" (verse 29; cf. Isa. 13:6-11; Joel 2:31; 3:15; and note the later but similar prophecy in Rev. 6:12-17, all of which are generally accepted by evangelical commentators as being signs of the *parousia*). The most definite fulfillments of these signs were in 1780 and 1833, after the tribulation, or long years of persecution of Christians by both pagan and papal powers.

Jesus did not foresee the reformation of humankind in response to the approaching end. He rather compared men's reactions to those of the contemporaries of Noah and Lot, who ignored the signs of their time, rejected appeals for repentance and reformation, continued in their godless ways, and perished by water or by fire, while the godly few were spared. In making the analogy between those times and the years preceding His own return, the Lord declared, "Even thus shall it be in the day when the Son of man is revealed" (Luke 17:26-30).

The reactions of those who reject or are indifferent to Christian standards do not surprise those who look for the Second Coming, but the condition of those whose Christianity is formal and shallow causes fraternal spiritual concern, though that condition itself is a sign of the last days. It must amaze the heavenly family that professed members of the Christian church remain so unmoved by the prospect of their Master's return that they hold on to their unsanctified traits with one hand while hopefully clinging to their shreds of spirituality with the other. Yet this is the state within the last-day church as perceived by Paul and expressed in 2 Timothy 3:1-5, where he describes those "who put pleasure in the place of God, men who preserve the outward form of religion, but are a standing denial of its reality" (verses 4, 5, N.E.B.). May we allow the Spirit to preserve us from such a useless mockery of true religion!

Signs of Return—III

It is dangerously easy for the human mind to concentrate on the concrete and to neglect the reflective. Jesus did not fall into that error: He gave balanced attention to both aspects of all the subjects He touched. When informing His followers of the signs of His return, He dealt also with their effect on the minds of those who observed them. After announcing "signs in the sun, and in the moon, and in the stars," He foretold distress and perplexity among the nations, and observed that "men's hearts [would be] failing them for fear" because of the peace-shattering events that were coming upon them (Luke 21:25, 26).

To all Christians of all ages the Saviour addresses solemn counsel. "Take heed to yourselves," He advises (verse 34), but He does not thereby advocate a "save yourself" program. He is rather recommending self-examination because of the spiritual dangers that will confront His followers in the troubled times that precede His coming. Are we surprised, even shocked, at the warning? We should be, for it deals with some topics that ought never to trouble a Christian—dissipation (surfeiting) and drunkenness. The most effective solution to those problems is prevention by temperance in eating good food, even at festive times, and total abstinence from all intoxicating drinks, making drunkenness in any form a nonevent.

The third peril mentioned by Jesus is "cares of this life," or everyday worries. In one sense these cannot be avoided, and their number will increase as times become more troubled. But their impact can be lessened, even minimized, by avoidance of gluttony and rejection of intoxicants, disciplines that yield clearer minds capable of handling daily anxieties, a regimen that produces *mens sana in corpore sano*, a sound mind in a sound body. Those who look for our Lord's appearing should be among the foremost exemplars of these Christian temperance principles.

An urgency in applying these counsels arises from the passage of time. One and one-half centuries have passed since the spectacular fall of stars in 1833, a short space on the divine time scale, but the length of two or three normal human lives, bringing us significantly nearer to the coming of our King. We need to be aware of the danger of being taken unawares (Luke 21:34), remembering that "'that day will close on you unexpectedly like a trap'" (verse 34, N.I.V.). Safety, according to the King Himself, lies in spiritual preparedness. "Be on the alert, praying at all times for strength to pass safely through all these imminent troubles and to stand in the presence of the Son of Man" (verse 36, N.E.B.).

WE
BELIEVE
IN

"THY KINGDOM
COME"

As we have just reminded ourselves, the King is coming! Now we want to express our relief, our joy, at the momentous news by offering the prayer, "Thy kingdom come." The news and the prayer are inseparable, just as are the King and His kingdom, for there is no effective king without a kingdom and no kingdom without a king.

Because our chapter title forms part of the most famous of all prayers, its petition probably has been repeated more than any other. But how many of us consciously pray for the coming of Christ's kingdom when we join in the congregational offering of the prayer? Yet this must be what Jesus intended. The request is an integral and essential part of the complete petition, which is filled from beginning to end with concern for the kingdom of God. It may be said to center on two personalities—the King and His subjects, who can achieve their full potential only within the limitless bounds of that eternal realm. When, therefore, we seriously pray, "Thy kingdom come," we are pledging our allegiance to the King, offering our services for the reestablishment of divine rulership over every creature and all territory in heaven and on earth.

Jesus saw all this and much more when He came "preaching the gospel of the kingdom of God," and proclaiming, "The kingdom of heaven is at hand" (Mark 1:14; Matt. 4:17). The purpose of His ministry was to represent that kingdom so persuasively that men and women would want to become its citizens and to make it possible for that wish to be fulfilled by their being released from slavery to sin and being enlisted in the King's service. This explains the more than forty references to "the kingdom of heaven" or "the kingdom of God" in Matthew's Gospel alone. His Father's realm was the goal on which the Son's eyes were fixed. He returned to His celestial home "to prepare a place" for His people and to come again and receive them unto Himself. Therein lies the reason for His emphasis on the Second Advent—it will inaugurate the kingdom of God by bringing all its subjects into the royal domain, first in heaven, then on the renovated earth. Then will be answered our Lord's prayer, composed for us—"Thy kingdom come."

When?—I

No matter from which angle we approach the subject of our Lord's return, we soon come face to face with the same question that gripped the disciples' minds: "When shall these things be? and what shall be the sign of thy coming, and of the end of the world?" (Matt. 24:3). The Master's answer should lead us to be cautious on the topic: "Take heed that no man deceive you" (verse 4), either into too early or too late an expectation. In Biblical prophecy apart from the Gospels and in His own instruction Jesus has given a fund of information which, when carefully studied, is capable of alerting us to the nearness of His coming. There would be no point in the progressive buildup of predictions if they did not inform the relevant generation of the time when it might expect to "see the Son of man coming in the clouds of heaven with power and great glory."

In response to His listeners' interest in the date of His return, Jesus used an illustration that reflects the general rather than the specific nature of His instruction. He speaks of the fig tree's response to the approach of summer and applies that to the nearness of the end (Matt. 24:32-35). This interpretation holds, whether we accept the translation "it is near," or the valid alternative "he is near" in verse 33, for the whole trend of the following verses points to the "day and hour," to the "coming of the Son of man," and the hour when our Lord shall come (verses 36, 37, 39, 42, 44). Since Jesus speaks only of nearness and does not define "this generation" (verse 34), it is clear that we should not attempt a more precise dating for His return. This limitation should not weaken our expectation of His appearing, however, for He on whom our whole faith depends gives the firm assurance that His words—that is, His promises—shall never pass away (verse 35).

When?—II

In spite of the Lord's refusal to set a date for His second coming, the human heart hankers after a definitive time for the climactic event. In recognition but rejection of this desire, Christ affirmed the certainty of His return but no less clearly asserted that His Father was the only One who knew the day and hour of that coming. As we would say, a date had been set, but it was classified information, kept by the Father in His own omniscient mind, where even the Son Himself was content to leave it (see Mark 13:32). The Godhead knew that if men were told the day and hour, they would procrastinate in matters of repentance and evangelism and would leave vital spiritual decisions until the moment before the end and would find they had left them until too late. In this instance, then, our lack of knowledge safeguards us, and if the Lord of glory and His angels did not know the exact timing of the coming, who are we to demand such knowledge?

Jesus draws a positive lesson from our not knowing the precise hour of His return by comparing the experience with the situation that confronted the antediluvian world. Neither Noah nor his contemporaries knew the day when the deluge would begin, but Noah and his family were in a continual state of readiness, and before the rains came they had entered the ark and saved their lives. We are similarly situated, knowing that "the end of all things is at hand," yet not knowing when it will occur. "Watch, therefore," our Lord urges us, "for ye know not what hour your Lord doth come. . . . Be ye also ready" (Matt. 24:42-44). Our danger is even greater than that of Noah's generation. His contemporaries never knew Jesus of Nazareth; we know that the Son of God has come and is coming again soon and that there will be no possibility of salvation for any unrepentant soul at or after His appearing. We must be ready *before* He appears.

Why?

Our Master's second coming has a similar and closely related purpose to that which prompted His incarnation, namely that "rebellion shall be stopped, sin brought to an end, iniquity expiated, everlasting right ushered in, vision and prophecy sealed, and the Most Holy Place anointed" (Dan. 9:24, N.E.B.). What the first coming began, the Second Coming will complete.

But the divine design can never be fulfilled until all whom Heaven knows will accept His proffered salvation will have heard the good news and will have confessed their sins and been cleansed from all unrighteousness. This calls for the universal proclamation of the facts of salvation, which include the saving life, death, resurrection, and kingly return of Christ. The disciples learned this from their Lord's lips when He told them, "This gospel of the kingdom shall be preached in all the world for a witness unto all nations; and then shall the end come" (Matt. 24:14).

To those who first heard this proposal it must have

seemed a noble but impracticable vision. Their combined ministry had hardly scratched the surface of Palestine, so what hope was there of its reaching the whole world? But if that was their initial reaction, it came before the resurrection and was short-lived. Before the ascension they heard the same beloved voice commissioning them to fulfill His vision, to go "into all the world, and preach the gospel to every creature," to "teach all nations . . . to observe all things whatsoever I have commanded you" Mark 16:15; Matt. 28:19, 20). And they knew this was to be no impersonal preaching of a formal message, for it was to convict its hearers of sin and salvation and lead them to baptism and eternal life. So "they went forth, and preached every where, the Lord working with them" (Mark 16: 20).

The result of this inspired witness was an amazingly widespread dissemination of the gospel within the apostles' lifetimes. They and their converts "went every where preaching the word" (Acts 8:4; 11:19), until much of the then known world had been reached.

Then came a lull as the church lost its first love and thereby its urge to share the gospel with its fellow human beings. Yet in spite of lukewarmness the number of believers grew until much of the Mediterranean world and Europe became nominally Christian but increasingly inward-looking, self-centered, even through the Reformation era. It was not until the eighteenth century that a missionary conscience again awoke and prepared the way for the nineteenth century global missionary movement.

Today the church faces the danger of foundering on the rocks of demography. The astounding population growth leaves the baptismal rate far, far behind and confronts the church with a spiritual and ecclesiological problem that will not disappear with a wave of a preacher's hand. Millions upon millions have no adequate chance to hear the gospel and no opportunity to acknowledge Him as their Lord and their God. And the number of the unreached increases every day. With the Lord's "not [being] willing that any should perish, but that all should come to repentance" (2 Peter 3:9), we are challenged with a task of staggering proportions.

How?—I

The preceding paragraph leaves us with an unanswered question, but since these are doctrinal and not administrative studies, we continue our consideration of the Advent and ask how our Lord will come; and on that subject we have abundant Biblical information.

As Christ sat on the slopes of Olivet and gave His chosen twelve a glimpse into the future, He faced the problem of describing the unseen in words that are tied to the visible. The realities were so vast that when they were conveyed in a few earth-bound words, foreshortening and omission were inevitable. When we allow for these limitations and when we avoid too literalistic an interpretation, the Saviour's revelations unveil even more glories than those we first perceived.

The simplest point of departure is near Bethany, where "two men . . . in white apparel" stand by the apostles and announce, "This same Jesus, which is taken up from you into heaven, shall so come in like manner as ye have seen him go into heaven" (Acts 1:10, 11). Since a cloud had just "received him out of their sight" (verse 9), it is reasonable to conclude that He will return with a cloud.

This conclusion is supported by other scriptures, from some of Christ's earliest recorded words on the topic to the final vivid pictures drawn in the Apocalypse. "The Son of man . . . shall come in his own glory, and in his Father's, and of the holy angels," Luke records (chap. 9:26; cf. Matt. 13:41; 16:27; Mark 8:38). Later the Lord speaks of "the sign of the Son of man in heaven" when "they shall see the Son of man coming in the clouds of heaven with power and great glory" (Matt. 24:30). He repeats this during His trial before Caiaphas when He declares, "Hereafter shall ye see the Son of man sitting on the right hand of power, and coming in the clouds of heaven" (chap. 26:64). In Matthew 24:31 and 25:31 angels are again brought into the picture, and we see them augmenting the cloud of glory around the returning Lord (see *Early Writings*, p. 286).

What Christ foresaw, Paul caught in vision. There is a majesty in his portrayal of the Son's descent from heaven "with a shout, with the voice of the archangel, and with the trump of God," and of "the Lord Jesus . . . revealed from heaven with his mighty angels" (1 Thess. 4:16; 2 Thess. 1:7). He who had met the risen Lord on the Damascus road was better prepared than most for the triumphant glory of His second coming.

How?—II

Instruction concerning our Lord's return is not restricted to the New Testament but finds a place in even earlier times. According to Jude, who appears to be quoting from the First Book of Enoch, a noncanonical writing known among Jews by the first century B.C., the patriarch Enoch prophesied that "the Lord cometh with ten thousands of his saints" (Jude 14; see *The Seventh-day Adventist Bible Commentary*, on Jude 14). The psalmist expresses his conviction that "our God shall come, and shall not keep silence; a fire shall devour before him" (Ps. 50:3), and many commentators read this as a reference to Christ's coming. Isaiah, while not attempting to describe the physical aspects of the Advent, does depict the effect of the appearing upon those who have been faithfully awaiting it (chap. 25:8, 9). Daniel speaks of "one like the Son of man" who "came with the clouds of heaven" (Dan. 7:13), and although the time frame may not be as clear as some might think, the picture closely resembles Christ's own account of His return. It is also possible to see in Habakkuk's vision (chap. 3:3-6) a preview of the awe-inspiring spectacle of the Lord's procession from heaven toward earth at the time of His glorious appearing.

To round out the Biblical prospectus of the Parousia, we turn to "the revelation of Jesus Christ, which God gave unto him [John]." The whole Apocalypse is Second Coming conscious, constantly anticipating the opening of the heavens, eager to see the King of kings and Lord of lords on a white horse, followed by His heavenly hosts, riding into a sinless future. From the first chapter with its announcement, "Behold, he cometh with clouds" (Rev. 1:17), to the last, with its double assurance, "Behold, I come quickly" and "Surely I come quickly" (chap. 22:12, 20), the momentum of its prophetic recital carries it inexorably into the eternity where "the Lord God omnipotent reigneth" (chap. 19:6). Its theme song is its own alleluia chorus (chap. 11:15; 19:6). Its plea to its King is, "Even so, come, Lord Jesus" (chap. 22:20).

How to Be Ready

This subtitle's topic cannot be restricted to one subject, for it must apply to the entire range of Christian doctrine with its intrinsic appeal to prepare for eternity. But no conscientious study of the Second Coming can evade consideration of the Master's admonition, "Be ye also ready" (Matt. 24:44), which forms the climax of His instruction on His coming and is supported by other New Testament writers in similar contexts.

How shall we prepare? Christ's immediate answer is, "Watch therefore" (Matt. 24:42), or more literally, "Keep awake" or "Be on the alert," because we do not know the time of His return. This suggests the danger of our growing lax as time passes. In the same breath it confirms the certainty of His coming, even when we least expect it (verse 44). The truth is that we must so live that no matter when our Lord appears we shall be ready and waiting for Him, with lives that witness to our having been saved by His grace.

Christ struck the note of need for preparation. His ministers have followed His lead, from the days of Pentecost onward (e.g., Acts 2:37-40; 3:19, 20; 2 Cor. 5:14, 15). Awareness of the Advent should have a profound effect on our everyday lives and our relationships with others. Christian Hebrews learned this from their own Epistle (chap. 10:24, 25), and their contemporary fellow believers doubtless shared similar counsel. All Adventists—that is, all who expect the return of Christ in glory—must accept the spiritual responsibility that goes with such a belief. Says Peter, "Since the whole universe is to break up in this way, think what sort of people you ought to be, what devout and dedicated lives you should live! . . . Do your utmost to be found at peace with him, unblemished and above reproach in his sight" (2 Peter 3:11-14, N.E.B.).

WE
BELIEVE
IN

ALL THINGS NEW

Few will dispute the need for renovations. Thousands of years of wrongdoing, of abuse of natural resources, of progressive pollution of air, land, and water, and persistent debasement of human nature leave no alternative for the One in whose hands rests the welfare of our world and of the universe.

In the face of that misuse the everyday sense of the word *renovate* does not meet the need that confronts the Creator. The stricter meaning of the word is required, for all things must indeed be made new. A mere refurbishing of the old will not suffice; a new creation is called for, and Scripture promises that it will come.

When Lucifer, aided and abetted by newly created humanity, sabotaged the perfection of Eden, it would have been easy (as we might say) for the Almighty to have scrapped His plans for our planet and to have made a new world to replace the one that had so quickly come to grief. But such action would have been contrary to His nature, and He chose to adhere to the original plan by defeating evil on its own chosen battleground and by restoring the earth to its pristine sinless glory.

The divine purpose was revealed (Gen. 3:15) even before the first human sinners were sent out of Eden, and hope of its fulfillment animated them and their descendants throughout the patriarchal years and into the times of the major and minor prophets. The clearest vision was first given to Isaiah as he foresaw the

restoration of Edenic conditions under the reign of
Christ (Isa. 11:1-10; 25:8, 9; 35; 65:17-25) and perceived
that He intended to "create new heavens and a new
earth" (chap. 65:17). Even Jeremiah, amid his anguish
over the destruction of his beloved Jerusalem, looked
ahead to more glorious days and saw a King, the
righteous Lord, once again reigning over His people
(chap. 23:5, 6). Then came Daniel, exiled in Babylon but
seeing the end of earthly monarchies and the establishment of the eternal kingdom under "the God of heaven"
and One like a son of man, "an everlasting dominion,
which shall not pass away" (chap. 2:44; 7:13, 14).

When the Son of man would come, firsthand
knowledge of the new kingdom would come with Him.

Assured Inheritance

It is not easy for impatient human beings to believe
in the fulfillment of God's original plans. We can see the
beauty of the first design and see the logic of its
restoration, but we are by nature impatient for its
completion and grow weary of waiting for the consummation. To all such impatient and wondering ones the
Creator gives this assurance: "The Lord shall be king
over all the earth" (Zech. 14:9). "The saints of the most
High shall take the kingdom, and possess the kingdom
for ever" (Dan. 7:18). In consequence, peace and
stability will reign forever; crude might shall not be
right. "In his days shall the righteous flourish" (Ps.
72:7), and at long last "the meek shall inherit the earth;
and shall delight themselves in the abundance of peace"
(Ps. 37:11), a commodity they have not often enjoyed in
this present world.

But first those foresights must be realized and those
promises fulfilled. This, according to Biblical teaching,
depends on the success of Christ's mission.

The three Synoptic Gospels agree in reporting
Christ's opening work to be the preaching of "the gospel

of the kingdom of God" (Mark 1:14; Matt. 4:17; cf. Luke 4:16-19). That note, once struck, reverberated throughout His whole ministry. It rang through His words and His deeds. In words it found early expression in the Sermon on the Mount (Matt. 5:3, 10, 19, 20; 6:10, 13, 33; 7:21) and was later the central theme in many of His parables (chap. 13). He never lost sight of that central objective. It figured in the daily service to His compatriots (chap. 9;35), in the training of His disciples (chap. 16:19; 26:29), in His teaching about future events (chap. 24:14; 25:34), and even in the last human words addressed to Him on the cross (Luke 23:42, 43). At many times and in many ways the evangelists reveal that the kingdom of heaven was central in their Master's thinking.

The Geography of Heaven

We should observe, however, that the Lord says very little about the physical aspects of that kingdom. Apart from John 14:1-3, with its reference to accommodations in His Father's house, the emphasis is largely spiritual, stressing character requirements for entrance into the kingdom of heaven (see Matt. 7:21; 18:1-4). Indeed, we must not lightly equate the new earth and the New Jerusalem with the kingdom, for the Saviour's teaching would suggest a wider interpretation for the latter. He leaves more concrete descriptions of the life to come to later New Testament writers who served the early church long after its Founder had returned to His celestial home. This may have been partly due to the pioneer nature of His ministry: He was breaking uncultivated soil and could observe to Nicodemus, "If I have told you earthly things, and ye believe not, how shall ye believe, if I tell you of heavenly things?" (John 3:12). Yet in spite of that recognition, He declined to satisfy idle curiosity about the geography of heaven and construction in it, realizing that few, if any, in His audiences were ready for the revelations that He was so well equipped to give.

They Seek a Country

Beyond any doubt, however, the Lord's brief ministry aroused, especially in the minds of His dearest friends, a healthy curiosity about the future life and an ardent desire to enjoy it in His incomparable company. Under this stimulus and the Spirit's guidance, they reviewed the past, looked into the future and brought us a wealth of revelation about the life that lies beyond death for those who trust in the Lord for salvation.

The writer of the long letter to the Hebrews, being very well versed in Old Testament history, had little difficulty in relating patriarchal experiences to his readers' situations in the first century A.D. In the course of his historical review (Heb. 11:4-40) he considered the faith of Abraham, whom he described as looking "for a city which hath foundations, whose builder and maker is God" (verse 10). This makes him a farsighted believer whose faith enabled him to look beyond his goatskin tent, beyond the fortifications of Salem and its successor, Jerusalem, to the celestial city we know as New Jerusalem. The vision of the Abrahamic family was even broader; it embraced "a country," that is, a fatherland, a home country of their own (verse 14), "an heavenly" (verse 16), since in Palestine they were no more than strangers and pilgrims. In so doing, they set a pattern for those who followed, giving them the heavenly uplook and fixing their eyes on the unseen, which is eternal, rather than on the visible, which is temporal (verses 13, 16).

In a somewhat similar way Peter leads his readers through patriarchal times, particularly those of Noah, and moves ahead to "the day of the Lord" when "the heavens shall pass away with a great noise, and the elements shall melt with fervent heat, the earth also and the works that are therein shall be burned up" (2 Peter 3:10). Then the apostle, with Abraham and the faithful, "according to his [the Lord's] promise, look for new heavens and a new earth" (verse 13). There is the age-old vision held by God-fearing redeemed people whose wanderings are over; who, having sought a country, have found it, and the city, and the universe, freed from the blight of sin, where they can worship and serve their Lord forever.

New Heaven, New Earth

When we look for graphic descriptions of the new earth, we turn to the last pages of our Bibles. It is as if the beloved disciple knew that his book would close the sacred canon, for what more fitting conclusion to Holy Writ could be found than chapters 21 and 22 of Revelation? They bring us up to and over the threshold of eternity. They give the most realistic glimpses of "the king in his beauty"; they enable us to behold enticing reaches of "the land that is very far off" (Isa. 33:17). Those two chapters merit careful and reverent, but restrained, study with the realization that they can present the unseen only in terms of the seen, the unknown in terms of the known, and they are consequently limited by our restricted knowledge. We might even murmur, in Cecil Rhodes' style, "So little known, so much to know!"—but with this consolation: We have before us an eternity in which to increase our knowledge.

With that humbling realization and stimulating prospect ahead, let us set out the main outline of John's vision of the new heaven and new earth.

First we should remind ourselves that John is on the Isle of Patmos, describing scenes he has seen in vision, recording some of what he has heard while he was "in the Spirit," and that he is still trying to share with his distant readers, in writing and in human language, the principal features of the revelations that have been granted him. At this final juncture he is shown the consummation of the great controversy, with sin defeated and abolished, with righteous unity eternally assured, and with God the Father, God the Son, and God the Spirit ruling a sinless universe, as originally planned.

The apostle sees that the first heaven and earth, as we know them, have passed away. They have both been tainted by sin. They need to be replaced, for restoration to the first condition as they were before Lucifer's rebellion will not suffice. The facts of sin, seen in the nail and spear prints and heard in the praises of those who have been redeemed from their sins, will not just go away, though they will not morbidly haunt God's family.

To replace the old there will be the new (Greek *kainos*). "By using the word *kainos,* John is probably emphasizing the fact that the new heavens and earth will be created from the purified elements of the old, and thus be new in quality, different. The new heavens and the new earth are, then, a re-creation, a forming anew of existing elements, and not a creation *ex nihilo.*"—*The SDA Bible Commentary,* on Rev. 21:1.

God With Us

The re-creation of our earth is not enough, for it would then be merely an uninhabited planet. John, therefore, is shown "the holy city, new Jerusalem, coming down from God out of heaven" (Rev. 21:2). The old Jerusalem has been destroyed by the brightness of the Second Coming and by the fires that have purified the earth and helped to make it new. In its place the New Jerusalem, where the redeemed have doubtless been spending the thousand years with Christ, descends from God out of heaven, "prepared as a bride adorned for her husband." How can a city be a bride? By this imagery the

seer informs us that the city is inhabited by the saints
who form the church, which is the bride of Christ (cf.
Eph. 5:22-32; Rev. 19:7, 8; 21:9, 10). In this way the
renewed earth will be populated by a people who have
overcome sin by the blood of the Lamb, that is, by faith
in Christ's sacrifice and by the strength He imparts.

While John marveled at the glory of the Holy City, he
"heard a great voice out of heaven saying, Behold, the
tabernacle of God is with men" (Rev. 21:3). Those
simple words form one of the most stupendous
announcements ever uttered through all eternity. The
great God, the Almighty, transfers His seat of government from heaven to earth. He who dwells "in the light
which no man can approach unto; whom no man hath
seen, nor can see" (1 Tim. 6:16), He will ultimately
dwell with those whom He has saved.

There is a holy significance in John's use of the Greek
words for "tabernacle" and "dwell," which are from the
verb *skēnoō*, "to live, to dwell," the noun form being
skēnē, "tent" or "tabernacle." The same verb is used by the
same author in John 1:14, where he literally says, "And the
word became flesh and *tabernacled* among us." And now,
in the new world and in its capital city, the Lord God
tabernacles with His people, even as, under much
humbler circumstances, His Son had tabernacled among
His chosen but wayward people. The Edenic idyll when
He had walked in the Garden in the cool of the day and its
sequel when He lived with His own, though they received
Him not, is crowned—and eclipsed—by having both
Father and Son enthroned in the Holy City with its myriad
sinless inhabitants. What greater glory could come to any
capital and to any people? Having established this
awe-inspiring certainty, all of eternity's other wonders
flow from it in an ineffable array of never-ending blessings,
not the least of which is that "God himself shall be with
them, and be their God." "And they shall see his face"
(Rev. 21:3; 22:4).

Citizens of the Kingdom

Contemplation of the beauty and delights of the kingdom of heaven, which will come at last to earth, will be tantalizing and frustrating unless we ourselves can be assured of enjoying its citizenship. How can we gain that assurance?

The answer comes from Him "that sat upon the throne," and He says, "He that overcometh shall inherit all things" (Rev. 21:5, 7). This answer tallies with the formula given to the faithful in each of the seven churches (chapters 2 and 3). To each such overcomer a separate promise is given that can find complete fulfillment only in the new earth, the paradise of God (chap. 2:7 ff.). The final reward, promised not in anticipation as are the others, but at the time of realization, comes to the same kind of people, those who keep on overcoming.

The simplistic explanation of the term "overcomer" refers to the conquest of one's own weaknesses, of everyday temptations and, without doubt, this type of victory is essential. But there is also a more dramatic definition, given in Revelation 12:11: "They overcame him [the devil, verse 9] by the blood of the Lamb, and by the word of their testimony; and they loved not their lives unto the death." They engage in the life-and-death struggle against the author of evil and prevail "by the blood of the Lamb," that is, by virtue of Christ's victory on the cross, wherein lies the only source of hope for victory for any of us. In addition, they bear courageous witness to their convictions, even to the point of dying rather than denying their faith. This is the quality of Christians who will become citizens of the eternal kingdom, of whom the Father will say, "I will be his God, and he shall be my son" (Rev. 21:7).

One other notable prerequisite is cited for citizenship. It is conveyed by the Alpha and Omega Himself when He says, "Blessed are they that do his commandments [or, "that wash their robes"], that they may have right to the tree of life, and may enter in through the gates into the city" (chap. 22:14). This is a reasonable and essential requirement, for the peace of the kingdom would be shattered if any of its inhabitants refused to observe the King's laws or had not washed their robes, that is, transformed their characters in the blood of Jesus Christ, which cleanses from all sin.

The standards are understandably high for so high an estate but, with Paul, we can say, "I can do all things through Christ which strengtheneth me" (Phil. 4:13). The outcome, therefore, lies in our own wills, in our own readiness to use the strength our Saviour offers.

WE
BELIEVE
IN

CHRISTIANITY AND
HEALTH

Although health plays such a vital part, literally, in everyone's life, although it has profound effects on spiritual well-being, and although it receives significant attention in the Bible, the topic gets little notice from the majority of Christian churches. Seventh-day Adventists are among the few who afford it a prominent and honored place in their teachings. This is a scriptural attitude. The Bible shows a concern for the whole man: body, soul, and spirit, or the physical, spiritual, and mental welfare of each member of the human family. It is therefore right for Bible-believing Christians to hold a doctrine that relates health to the practice of religion.

When we recognize the Bible's interest in our physical well-being, we should also perceive the converse implications of that interest, namely, our responsibility toward God in matters relating to health. That is part of the balanced, holistic view of life and religion that has always been embedded in Old and New Testament writings. The Creator did not make man by bringing together independent parts and pieces, but "formed man of the dust of the ground, and breathed into his nostrils the breath of life; and man became a living soul" (Gen. 2:7), complete, indivisible, with neither body nor spirit able to subsist apart from the other. From this it follows that the welfare of the one is closely related to the welfare of the other.

Such an analysis lies behind Paul's counsel to his

converts in Corinth as he advised them, "Whether therefore ye eat, or drink, or whatsoever ye do, do all to the glory of God" (1 Cor. 10:31). They were to realize that every department of their lives was to be touched by their responsibility toward God. No section could be roped off, sealed from the influence and control of their newfound Christianity. All their daily actions, even those of eating and drinking, were to contribute to God's glory.

God's Ideal for His Children

The Christian concept of Creation has a profound influence not only on its philosophy of origins but also on that of the end, or objective, of human life. The belief that "God created man in his own image" (Gen. 1:27) inseparably links men to God, provides him with the highest possible ideal, and places upon him unrelenting moral responsibilities. Within certain inherent limitations, man is to be like God, especially in respect to character. Just as God so effectively provides His own self-discipline so that He needs none, having no inordinate desires that need control or conquest, so He created man with the capability of attaining perfect holiness. At the same time He gave man free will, the power of choice that enables him to emulate and serve either God or the devil.

If Eve and Adam had resisted the first temptation, which was couched in terms of appetite, they would have been fortified against further weakness, for as the temperance hymn tells us, "Each victory will help you some other to win." But the first pair yielded instead of resisting and went downward in sinfulness instead of upward in holiness. Their descendants have been monotonously repeating that pattern in their own experiences.

The Creator, loving His creation with an everlasting love, has never left men and women to their own devices. He has ever wanted to save them from the results of their own folly and to bring them back to His original ideal. To this end He gave His chosen people detailed instruction on medical and sanitary matters, promising that if they followed His counsel, doing "that which is right in his sight," giving "ear to his commandments," and keeping "all his statutes," they would avoid the diseases that plagued the Egyptians. His love for Israel led Him to care for their physical health as well as for their social freedom and spiritual well-being. He even described Himself as "the Lord that healeth thee" (Ex. 15:26; cf. Deut. 7:12-15) and promised to "bless thy bread, and thy water; and I will take sickness away from the midst of thee" (chap. 23:25).

There can be no doubt about the Lord's interest in His people's health. He wants to heal all our diseases and to keep us youthful (Ps. 103:3, 5), though our inherited and cultivated tendencies often make it difficult and sometimes impracticable for Him to fulfill those benevolent intentions.

Guidance on Diet

The origin of God's concern for every detail of His children's lives derives from His great love and His desire to see them develop to the best of their potential. "Higher than the highest human thought can reach is God's ideal for His children."—*Education*, p. 18. For them He has lofty ambitions: "For thou art an holy people unto the Lord thy God, and the Lord hath chosen thee to be a peculiar people unto himself, above all the nations that are upon the earth" (Deut. 14:2). He saw what they could become under His tutelage. The depth of His love can be gauged by realizing that He also knew what a disappointing people they would continue to be.

In spite of the Israelites' frailties, the Lord gave them the information that would enable them to remain far healthier than their neighbors. This was the purpose behind the guidance concerning clean and unclean foods recorded in Leviticus 11 and Deuteronomy 14:3-21, and since the physiology and habits of the listed creatures have not changed, the counsel is as valid today as when it was given more than 3,000 years ago. We shall certainly lose no good thing in abiding by its precepts.

It is generally agreed that the question of total abstinence from intoxicating drink cannot be settled solely on a Biblical basis. While there were some who denied themselves whatever pleasures are reputed to come from alcoholic drinks, the general population used such beverages as far as their means would allow. With the ministry of Christ and the birth of Christianity came a more critical attitude toward social evils and a readiness to deny self in order to set an example that would lead others to eschew all kinds of strong drink.

The nineteenth and twentieth centuries have seen many brave temperance movements at work, but it must be confessed that none has made much impact on the continuing problem of drunkenness, which still ruins constitutions and characters and brings needless poverty, injury, brutality, and fear into the lives of alcoholics, their families, and other victims. In the face of such persistent evil the Christian can best help by practicing total abstinence himself and by encouraging others to do the same. He will thereby promote his own health and that of those who follow his example.

Jesus and Health

The definition of a Christian requires that he follow the example of the Founder of his religion in every department of life. In respect to health, that calls for him to emulate Christ's attitude toward ill health in others and to exercise restraint in his own habits for the benefit of his own health.

From the outset of His ministry Jesus showed

Himself to be the Great Physician. The first chapter of Mark's Gospel records this in the number of healing miracles that are there reported (Mark 1:21-45). Matthew summarizes the mercies of those early days by saying, "Jesus went about all Galilee, . . . healing all manner of sickness and all manner of disease among the people. And his fame went throughout all Syria" (Matt. 4:23, 24). The same evangelist later uses similar words to tell of the Saviour's continuing medical ministry among His suffering compatriots and reports that "when he saw the multitudes, he was moved with compassion on them" (chap. 9;35, 36). This led Him to ordain twelve disciples, giving them also "power . . . to heal all manner of sickness and all manner of disease," even as He Himself did (chap. 10:1).

As the apostles continued the merciful work their Lord had begun they too cared for the health of many of the invalids who heard the gospel from their lips (see Acts 3:1-11; 5:12-16; 8:5-8; 9:36-42). In succeeding centuries it has been Christian initiative that has founded hospitals, orphanages, old-age homes, and has shown loving, practical concern for millions who had been hitherto neglected. Today, the Master's commission still stands, though its practitioners must adapt to rapidly changing conditions in all corners of the earth, making differing types of contributions as basic medical needs are increasingly met by governmental agencies.

Jesus also wants us to consider our own health needs, for it would be tragic if we spent time and energy sharing the gospel of spiritual and physical health with others only to find ourselves unsaved. In expectation of His return He tells us to take care because we might be caught by the same traps that have ensnared others— dissipation, drunkenness, and everyday anxieties (Luke 21:34, 35). We may deny the very possibility of our being caught in such toils; but alas, the danger is all too real, and our Lord sees the need of warning us about it.

Faithfulness to Christian health principles will help to protect us from the snares that could destroy us.

The Believer and His Body

The Christian's body has not always been his pride. There have been eras when believers have looked upon the body as the enemy of the soul, and have used Paul's disclosure "I keep under my body, and bring it into subjection" (1 Cor. 9:27) as justification for mortifying their bodies in an attempt to conquer physical desires and attain deeper spirituality. But Paul knew better. He believed that the Christian's body and spirit had been bought at the price of Christ's death and must therefore be recognized as the temple of the Holy Spirit (chap. 6:19, 20). Acknowledgment of this solemn fact makes it obligatory for us to care for both body and spirit, that the Spirit might find in us an attractive sanctuary.

> "From sin and sorrow set us free,
> And make Thy temples worthy Thee."

The solution to the problem of ownership of our bodies and also our spirits lies in our acceptance and practice of Paul's further counsel given in Romans 12:1: "Present your bodies a living sacrifice, holy, acceptable unto God." Such a gift will make God the owner and manager of our bodies and the controller of their needs and desires. This may prove to be the secret of true health reform. It will surely lead us "to abstain from all intoxicating drinks, tobacco and other narcotics, and to avoid every body- and soul-defiling habit and practice."—*Church Manual,* "Fundamental Beliefs," paragraph 17, p. 37.

Spirit-Inspired Temperance

One aspect of the many-sided genius of Christianity is its refusal to be pressured into mechanistic interpreta-

tions and applications of its tenets. The God whom it
worships is "spirit," and one member of the Godhead is
named as "Spirit." Its adherents are admonished to
worship "in spirit and in truth" (John 4:23, 24), and the
whole trend of its teaching is profoundly spiritual, as
opposed to the earthiness of many other religions. At the
same time it is intensely practical. While its head is in
the clouds keeping contact with heaven, its feet are on
this earth, and its hands touch every department of our
daily lives.

The spiritual nature of Christian doctrine concerning health and temperance needs to be continually
recalled or the subject becomes merely medical and
should then be left in the hands of capable and
dedicated physicians. This, as Christian doctors agree,
should not be, since the doctrine concerns both soul and
body. The Biblical approach is primarily spiritual, as
may be seen in its record of Christ's miracles and those
of His apostles (e.g., Mark 2:5; John 11:4; Acts 3:6). It is
also revealed in apostolic counsel to early Christian
congregations who had to struggle against pagan
materialism and pseudospirituality.

These reminders have a direct bearing on a true
understanding of religion's relation to health. As
already noted, Paul urges us to give God our bodies as
part of our moral and spiritual adoration of the Most
Holy (Rom. 12:1). He clearly sees that we cannot
compartmentalize our religion, giving God what we
narrowly conceive as spiritual while retaining the
physical for our own delectation. There must be no such
dichotomy. If we persist, we shall find ourselves bereft
of the best of both.

Pauline thought in this respect is developed at
greater length in his letter to the Galatians, who were
struggling to maintain their Christianity against a
floodtide of legalism—a struggle in which we are also
engaged, willy-nilly. In chapter 5 he counsels us to

"walk in the Spirit," to "be led of the Spirit," instead of being motivated by barren legal considerations. He labels the latter as "works of the flesh" and contrasts them to "the fruit of the Spirit," thereby setting our sights on the moral issues that underlie our present topic of temperance and such mundane matters as eating and drinking (verses 16-23). These are irrevocably related to our spiritual health and ultimately to our salvation.

The solution to the struggle between flesh and spirit, says Paul to the Thessalonians, lies in allowing ourselves to be completely sanctified, set apart, made holy by God Himself. When we allow Him to do this for us, our whole "spirit and soul and body," our complete being, will "be preserved blameless unto the coming of our Lord Jesus Christ" (1 Thess. 5:23). And that is just what we, in our heart of hearts, really want, is it not?

Health for Evermore

Of the untold millions of God-fearing men and women who have lived, very few have been translated without seeing death, and not one of them has returned to describe the beauty of the "land of far distances" (Isa. 33:17, N.E.B.). That land has remained, in human reckoning, "the undiscover'd country from whose bourn no traveller returns." Even He who inhabited eternity, who left it for a few years and then returned to His Father's house—even He gave no description of its unimaginable glories. What little has been told us has come through prophets' visions—from Isaiah, Daniel, Paul, and John, to name the principal four—and each of them still awaits entrance into God's own country.

There are some certainties, however, on which we can fix our interest and our hope. They may be said to spring from the defeat of sin, which will no longer wreak its havoc on God's creatures and their environment. Since sin caused death, absence of sin spells the abolition of death and the possession of eternal life, though this must also be seen as the fulfillment of Christ's repeated promises, as for example in Luke 18:29, 30; John 3:16, 18, 36; 5:24; 6:40, 47; 10:27, 28; 11:25, 26. Restoration of eternal life is the delayed realization of the Godhead's original plan for mankind and was, as Jesus explained in His Good Shepherd discourse (John 10:10), the prime objective of His earthly ministry.

It would be inconceivable, and indeed impossible, for the redeemed to obtain eternal life while remaining subject to disease, for disease and death are inextricably related. The promise of everlasting life therefore carries with it the assurance of freedom from disease and the suffering it brings. In Zion, says Isaiah's prophecy, "the inhabitant shall not say, I am sick" (chap. 33:24), and the Revelator hears the assuring words, "There shall be no more death, neither sorrow, nor crying, neither shall there be any more pain" (Rev. 21:4). There will be health for evermore. What a reassuring prospect! What relief, what potential that will bring to the citizens of the Eternal City and the subjects of the eternal King!

WE
BELIEVE
IN

SPIRITUAL GIFTS

As is always the case in spiritual matters, our Exemplar is Jesus Christ. As the Holy Ghost came upon Mary and she conceived by the Spirit (Luke 1:35; Matt. 1:18, 20), so the Christian is to be "born of the Spirit" (John 3:5, 6). As at our Lord's baptism "the Holy Ghost descended in a bodily shape like a dove upon him" (Luke 3:22), so the newly baptized is promised "the gift of the Holy Ghost" (Acts 2:38). The parallels are too remarkable to ignore, though they should strike awe into the perceptive heart.

It should not surprise us that the Saviour needed the Spirit's cooperation for success in defeating the devil and rescuing men, women, and children from his clutches. The responsibility for salvation was a triple one, borne by Father, Son, and Spirit. The Son did not work in isolation, independently of the other two members of the Godhead, but operated closely with them and was supported by them throughout His redemptive mission.

When Jesus publicly announced His vocation to His fellow townsfolk in Nazareth, He invoked the Spirit's authority and endowment in the work He had just begun. He declared to His fellow citizens that "the Spirit of the Lord" had anointed Him to preach, to heal, to deliver, to restore sight, and to liberate (Luke 4:18). The sequel to that announcement was the miracle-working life of Him "who went about doing good, and healing all that were oppressed of the devil" (Acts 10:38).

Each Christian has been called to continue the work that his Lord so graciously began. That commission can be fulfilled only in the power of the Spirit by the giving and acceptance and employment of that selfsame Spirit's gifts.

Divine Partnership

If the Son of God needed to be empowered by the Spirit for His ministry, surely His followers, faulty and frail, wholly human as they are, also need to be endued with the Spirit's power, knowledge, guidance, and gifts for the fulfillment of the responsibilities the Master has placed upon them.

The need was foreseen. Jesus told His disciples on the night of His betrayal, "I will pray the Father, and he shall give you another Comforter [or, Helper, Advocate], that he may abide with you for ever; even the Spirit of truth." "But the Comforter, which is the Holy Ghost, . . . shall teach you all things" (John 14:16, 17, 26). That instruction was not to be brand-new. During the fleeting three years that they had been with Jesus the disciples had been taught in a deeper, higher, more concentrated way than had ever been the lot of other mortals. They had consorted with the Son of God, "whose goings forth have been from of old, from everlasting." They had not known what was lying ahead, but their Teacher did, and He trained them accordingly. And now that separation was near, He "opened . . . their understanding, that they might understand the Scriptures." Specifically, He explained to them the significance of His sufferings and resurrection in relation to "repentance and remission of sins" that "should be preached in his name among all nations, beginning at Jerusalem" (Luke 24:45-47; Acts 1:1-5).

The Master also knew that they were not naturally capable of remembering all that they heard from His lips. He therefore encouraged them with the further promise that the Spirit would recall to their remembrance "all things . . . whatsoever I have said unto you" (John 14:26). This supernatural recollection must be borne in mind when considering the writing of the Gospels, the exposition of the Scriptures, and the fruitful public ministry rendered by the apostles in the post-ascension years. It was the fruitage of the Spirit's constant tuition.

They, in turn, were to be "witnesses of these things," testifying in undreamed-of ways and on an unimagined scale of the soul-shaking experience that had come to them in personally knowing and living and working with the Holy One, the Son of the most high God.

Promise and Fulfillment

The eleven could hardly foresee the aloneness that would be theirs when their Lord returned to His heavenly home, but Jesus and the Father foreknew their state and planned to care for it through the ministry of the third person of the Godhead, the Holy Spirit. "He will guide you into all truth," they were promised. "He will shew you things to come. He shall glorify me" (John 16:13, 14). He would be their Guide as they continued the work Christ had begun. He would convince the world of its sin, of its need for Christ's righteousness, and of the inevitability of judgment (verses 7-11). They quickly learned that the Spirit would not do all this by Himself; they were to be His agents. In preparation for that role they were to tarry in Jerusalem until they were "endued with power from on high" (Luke 24:49). They waited, and the result was Pentecost, when "they were all filled with the Holy Ghost" (Acts 2:4).

Peter, the apostolic spokesman at the time, identified the Spirit's descent as fulfillment of Joel's prophecy concerning the last days. Sons and daughters, young men and old, menservants and maids were to receive unusual spiritual powers for the proclamation of the good news that centered on Jesus of Nazareth (verses 16-24). As Peter's audience perceived the fulfillment of the prophecy, about three thousand of them responded, were baptized, and began to share their newfound faith with the local Jews and those of the diaspora who were then thronging the Holy City. Some of those converts "consecrated their lives to the work of giving to others the hope that filled their hearts with peace and joy. They could not be restrained or intimidated by threatenings. The Lord spoke through them, and as they went from place to place, the poor had the gospel preached to them, and miracles of divine grace were wrought."— *The Acts of the Apostles,* p. 48.

The Spirit-guided Church

The vivid Lucan recital in his book the Acts of the Apostles reveals the secret of the amazing growth of the early church. They prayed, he tells us in chapter 4:31, and their prayers were so powerful that "the place was shaken where they were assembled together." The Holy Spirit came among them in response to their prayers, they individually came under His control, and as a result, "spake the word of God with boldness." They proclaimed God's word, not their own. They made known the fulfillment of prophecy in the saving ministry of Jesus of Nazareth, in the sending of the Holy Spirit, and in the transformation of their own lives. They demonstrated the reality of the Spirit's work by their unity, by their selfless sharing of possessions until they had all things in common (verse 32). The apostles, inspired by such dramatic evidence of promises fulfilled, "with great power gave . . . witness of the resurrection of the Lord Jesus," and as a direct result, "great grace was upon them all" (verse 33).

Subsequent experiences showed that the greatest gift of the Spirit was His own presence in the newly converted life. With that presence assured, all the outward proofs of His power followed irrepressibly. The career of Philip the deacon, as he left Jerusalem, went north to Samaria, preached Christ in that city, and healed many of its inhabitants (Acts 8:5-8), colorfully illustrated this. His success stirred Simon the sorcerer to envy. He coveted the power that flowed through Philip, and he perceived enough of its origin to be baptized, but without the Holy Spirit's taking possession of his soul (verses 9-16). When he saw the Spirit entering the lives of his fellow townspeople as apostolic hands were laid upon them, he envied them and tried to buy what they had received gratis by allowing the Spirit to possess them (verses 17-19). Peter had to rebuke him for his distortion of the Christian *modus operandi* and lead him to repent of his materialism (verses 20-24). "We cannot use the Holy Spirit. The Spirit is to use us. . . . But many will not submit to this. They want to manage themselves. This is why they do not receive the heavenly gift. . . . The power of God awaits their demand and reception. This promised blessing, claimed by faith, brings all other blessings in its train."—*The Desire of Ages*, p. 672.

Gifts in the Church

In the first fervor that arose from Pentecost it would appear that a great majority of converts opened their hearts to the indwelling Spirit. As year followed year, however, the initial white heat cooled and the spiritual quality of the church's members deteriorated. Pagan notions sought a foothold, and apostolic counsel and education were needed for the preservation of purity in belief and practice.

The Spirit's ministry was an inviting target for subversive teachings. In the Greco-Roman world many new Christians would come with an inheritance of pagan mystery religions and see in the work of the Holy

Spirit a reflection of their past spiritistic practices. Such neophytes needed clear instruction to enable them to differentiate between the true and the false and to gain a right understanding of the Spirit's function in the church.

In two notable passages, 1 Corinthians 12 and Ephesians 4:1-16, Paul carefully guides his congregations in this important area of Christian doctrine. His counsel erects a milestone on the road of church progress by defining and systematizing the gifts that the Spirit has provided in the church.

From the first and longer passage it is clear that there were misconceptions about the role of the Spirit's gifts and that these were weakening the cause. Paul purposes to correct error and to establish truth by examining the subject, particularly by stressing the lordship of God and the uniqueness of the Spirit's authority in all matters relating to the gifts (1 Cor. 12:5-7). He also emphasizes the variety of gifts and the authority of the Spirit in their distribution among church members, "dividing to every man severally [or, separately] as he [the Spirit] will," according to His divine wisdom and never at the whim of the church member (verse 11). The recipient, however, is responsible for the use he makes of any spiritual talent he has received; but the overriding consideration is always the welfare and unity of the church.

The Gift of Prophecy

The two listings of spiritual gifts from Paul's pen are not identical. In 1 Corinthians 12:28 he refers to apostles, prophets, teachers, miracles, healings, helps, governments, and diversities of tongues. In Ephesians 4:11 he lists apostles, prophets, and teachers, adds evangelists and pastors, and omits the five remaining gifts found in the Corinthian letter. From this it is clear that neither list is exhaustive. But apostles and prophets hold the first two places in each listing and are doubtless seen as occupying positions in church leadership. In the beginning an essential qualification for apostleship was that of having been one of the eleven disciples or, like Matthias, elected to replace Judas or, like Paul, dramatically chosen for a specialized ministry. By the end of the first century, however, the original holders of the office had all died and their mantles had been placed on other, less famous, shoulders, though the responsibilities of leadership were similar to those of their predecessors.

In addition to the first apostles, several prophets appear in the New Testament narrative, and there are no grounds for supposing that prophets were meant to disappear from church service in succeeding centuries. But Seventh-day Adventists, conscious of being called to global preaching of the three angels' messages of Revelation 14:6-12 to prepare the world for Christ's coming, believe they have been entrusted with a special manifestation of the prophetic gift in the work and writings of Ellen G. White (1827-1915). Scriptural support for the claim is found in Revelation 12:17, with its reference to "the woman," or church, and "the remnant of her seed, which keep the commandments of God, and have the testimony of Jesus Christ." Adventist belief in the continuing relevance of the Decalogue in Christian conduct is seen as fulfilling the first identifying feature of the remnant church; while "the testimony of Jesus" is interpreted in the light of Revelation 19:10, where the concluding phrase states, "The testimony of Jesus is the spirit of prophecy," which is taken to indicate the presence of the prophetic gift in the church in the last days.

Beyond dispute, Mrs. White has most faithfully and effectively fulfilled the role of a prophet in the Seventh-day Adventist Church. While living, she fearlessly guided the church through her spoken and written word. After death her voluminous writings have counseled and inspired the denomination and provided it with spiritual wisdom comparable only to that of the Bible itself.

But should we not remember that the Scriptures also promise us other spiritual gifts and that their Giver must surely expect us to use them too? Are they not also needed in the last-day complexities? "First apostles," said Paul, ". . . thirdly teachers" and the five other talents; "and some, evangelists; and some, pastors" (1 Cor. 12:28; Eph. 4:11). Why should we rob the church of potential power by neglecting the resources its Lord has given it?

The Greatest Gift

It is bafflingly easy to spend more time on one gift than all of the others combined, yet it may be stranger still to forget or to soft-pedal or to ignore the objective Paul had in mind when he so thoroughly discussed spiritual gifts with his fellow Christians. In concluding his exposition of the Spirit's gifts, he urges his readers to "covet earnestly the best gifts," or "ever seek to excel in the greater gifts" (1 Cor. 12:31, Weymouth), and then shows them "a more excellent way," the way of charity, or love.

The apostle has just been giving earnest attention to the gifts of tongues, of prophecy, and of knowledge, as given by the Spirit for the development of the church, but lays them all aside to concentrate upon the supreme and essential gift of love.

There is, of course, a reason for Paul's focusing upon a gift that he had not hitherto included among those that came from the Spirit. It is more than a gift. It is not a faculty like that of speaking in tongues, or of teaching, or of healing, or of prophesying, or even of apostleship. It is more than any of these. "Whether there be prophecies, they shall fail; whether there be tongues, they shall cease; whether there be knowledge, it shall vanish away." But love is a matter of being, of being like Him who is love, whose entire nature consists of love manifesting itself in myriad forms. Paul knew, no less than his fellow apostle John, that "God is love" and that all who wish to live with God must be permeated with that same superlative quality, must, in as great a degree as a transformed nature will permit, also be love.

As the thirteenth chapter of First Corinthians crowns the twelfth, so should Christian love crown the possession and practice of any spiritual gifts that might be bestowed upon us by the Spirit. Without that crown our other gifts may prove to be no more than "sounding brass, or a tinkling cymbal." God forbid that our lives should produce such useless sounds!

WE
BELIEVE
IN

CHRISTIAN
STEWARDSHIP

Even the best of words can get timeworn with constant usage until they become little more than clichés, conveniently used to cover a multitude of ideas and sometimes employed as camouflage for more disturbing and unwelcome thoughts that discretion would conceal. There are also fashions in words and phrases; some soon become dated and cry out to be discarded. There was a time, for instance, when "Systematic Benevolence" rang sweetly on many ears, but today it has a Victorian ring that makes it unacceptable to contemporary ears. "Christian Stewardship" may already be going the same way and may need replacement now or not much later.

These time-conditioned thoughts should not obscure the lasting value of the substance of which a title may conceal much and reveal little, for it is the substance and not the title that counts. In this chapter we need to recognize the indispensability of benevolence, the desirability of its being systematic, and the need for stewardship that is truly Christian in motivation and practice. We should also discern that God wants us to be rich. "Lay up for yourselves treasures in heaven," the Son of man tells us (Matt. 6:20), knowing that where our treasure is there our heart will also be. And we lose much by interpreting that solely in terms of ethereal wealth. Heaven is the depository where all true riches are found, and anyone who invests his wealth there is assured of the highest rates of interest and of perfect security.

How may we invest in such a sound venture? The procedure is analogous to the one we follow on earth: we restrain current expenditures in order to have more to invest in high-yielding stocks, bonds, or savings certificates. Our Celestial Adviser urges that we, for much better reasons, reduce our spending on earth in order to build a greater balance "where neither moth nor rust doth corrupt, and where thieves do not break through nor steal." Investment there is the most profitable step we can take here, if our belief holds any validity at all.

Creator and Owner

One of the innumerable beauties of our Christian religion is the way it touches on every aspect of our existence, and what it touches it refines and elevates. What, for example, could be more earth-bound than gardening? Yet the Bible reveals it as man's principal occupation in the perfection of Eden, where the Lord God placed him "to till it and care for it" (Gen. 2:15, N.E.B.). When our earth is restored to its original, perfect state, its inhabitants also "shall plant vineyards, and eat the fruit of them. . . . They shall not plant, and another eat" (Isa. 65:21, 22). None of this gardening program will be irksome, thanks to the character of the Creator and Owner of the property. He is the Landlord par excellence, thoughtful, skillful, ungrasping, generous to His servants, One for whom it is a delight to work. The Lord of Hosts is His name.

We need not—indeed we should not—wait until our arrival in Paradise before showing interest in the earth and its produce. Each one of us is now a steward of the good things that come from the earth. We may not welcome the office, but we cannot shrug off fulfillment of its responsibilities. Water, oil, air, gas, coal—all are part of the total gift of life that God gives to His creatures. In our hands lies a share in global ecology.

The fact that "the earth is the Lord's, and the fulness thereof" (Ps. 24:1) makes us more than gardeners and conservationists, good as those occupations are. It commissions us as God's agents for the welfare of our world and its peoples. In particular we are responsible for the church as the agency through which He educates and saves the human family. The local management of each section of that agency falls upon us as church members. This is the most onerous, and yet glorious, of a Christian's many duties.

Religion and Arithmetic

Our Creator's capacities must continually surprise those who thoughtfully consider them. Beyond the miracle of Creation itself lies the ongoing attention to detail, shared with His human intermediaries, for the direction of all departments of His people's lives, especially in areas of religious responsibility. No one man carried a heavier load in this area than did Moses, who shared with Israel the multitudinous details for the organization of its religious life after its exodus from Egypt. In theory this should not surprise us, for we know of the complexities of a snowflake and of an atom, yet our Lord's concern with the minutiae of religious organization still amazes us. The second half of Exodus, the books of Leviticus and Numbers, and much of Deuteronomy reveal His infinite capacity for taking pains, an ability that is often used for defining genius in man.

The instituting of tithe as a means of caring for the livelihood of the Levites is an illustration of God's care for those who devoted all their time to His service (Num. 18:21, 24). The Levites, in turn, were to make their own contribution by offering a tenth part of the tithes they received (verse 26). In this way the whole congregation of Israel had a part in the upkeep of the nation's spiritual life. No more equable and adequate distribution of communal responsibility has yet been devised. The Lord's use of arithmetic has stood the test of time.

The value of the tithing system is reflected in its longevity. It was known in Abrahamic days (Gen. 14:18-20), it was practiced by Jacob (Gen. 28:20-22), it was incorporated into the economy of Israel at the time of the Exodus (Lev. 27:30-33). But a century is a long time in human reckoning. Spiritual fervor grew slack, apostasy set in, and one of the early casualties was monetary support of religion. Five centuries, with all their vicissitudes, passed after the Exodus, and the practice of tithing fell on evil times until Hezekiah became king of Judah in about 725 B.C. and recalled his people to faithful support of the Temple, its services, and its priests. The Babylonian captivity just over a century later (586 B.C. and onwards) struck a bitter blow to Judah's religious practices, and it took Nehemiah's strong leadership to recall the exiles to faithful support of the priesthood when they did return to Jerusalem by 445 B.C.

But human memory is weak, and after a few years Malachi had to appeal to the nation to "bring . . . the tithes into the storehouse" (Mal. 3:10). In the New Testament are historical references to past payment of tithes (Heb. 7:4-9), but Christ's own mention of the custom takes the form of rebukes to scribes and Pharisees for their meticulous calculations for tithing while neglecting the exercise of weightier Christian virtues (Matt. 23:23; Luke 18:12). In so doing He was not condemning the tithing system but emphasizing a still higher duty—that of showing true Christian charity.

Christians face the same question that faces all religionists: How shall we finance the cause we have espoused? Apart from a few exotic plants, nothing lives on air alone, and even the simplest of human organizations need some support. No system yet devised can equal the even distribution of responsibility that is the genius of the tithing plan. It adheres to the scriptural principle of proportionate responsibility, "according to that a man hath, and not according to that he hath not," or, as the N.E.B. more simply expresses it: "God accepts what a man has; he does not ask for what he has not" (2 Cor. 8:12). Where much has been given, much is expected (Luke 12:48); but the common sin of covetousness often leads the rich to give proportionately much less of their wealth than the poor give of their pittances, as Jesus pointed out to His disciples as they saw the poor widow give "all that she had" (Mark 12:41-44).

The early church had ample opportunity to practice what its Founder taught. Many Christians in Judea were reduced to extreme poverty, and Paul appealed for help to other congregations. The Macedonian believers responded generously, not because they were wealthy, but out of "the abundance of their joy and their deep poverty," and thereby inspired other more affluent groups to liberality. This moved the apostle to recall the greatest instance of giving: "Ye know the grace of our Lord Jesus Christ, that, though he was rich, yet for your sakes he became poor, that ye through his poverty might be rich" (2 Cor. 8:9). Hard must be the heart and tightly closed must be the purse that remains untouched by this supreme example of unselfish generosity!

Throughout its two-thousand-year history, Christianity has seen its adherents struggle to resolve the problems raised by wealth and the possessions it brings. In its early days the question was settled by the members' having "all things common" (Acts 2:44) and by the itinerant and selfless nature of their leaders' lives, which prevented their becoming rich. But as the church grew older more of its members were drawn from the monied classes, and accumulation of wealth often weakened their dedication. There were periodic calls for a return to primitive godliness, and at intervals charismatic leaders tried to bring their followers back to

New Testament simplicity. St. Francis of Assisi (1182?-1226) was notable for his renunciation of wealth and his vows of complete poverty. But the struggle continued and is with us today.

The Son of man, poor as He personally was during His incarnation, did not condemn wealth or require all of His followers to renounce it. The balanced Christian ethic has recognized the responsibilities and pitfalls that come with riches and has emphasized the right use of money and possessions for the good of one's fellow creatures and the propagation of the gospel. It has approved voluntary poverty that springs from religious motives and discouraged avoidable poverty that is born of fecklessness, extravagance, drunkenness, gambling, and other unchristian habits.

Behind the church's attitude to her members' financial standings has been her Master's dictum, "A man's life consisteth not in the abundance of the things which he possesseth" (Luke 12:15), and His counsel, "Seek ye first the kingdom of God, and his righteousness; and all these things shall be added unto you" (Matt. 6:33). The Lord wished to share with all His followers His concern with priorities—the advancement of the kingdom of God and the possession of God's righteous character. When these two essentials are cared for, "all these things"—food, drink, clothing, the necessities of life that money buys—will be given us. Countless Christians have proved the Lord's promise to be true.

Religion and Others

Far too often talk of stewardship is limited to the use of money, and that is regrettable, for the subject is far deeper than dollars, pounds, francs, or any other currency. Cain put his finger on the true concern of stewardship when he impudently asked his Maker, "Am I my brother's keeper?" The answer was and still is

"Yes!" Each one of us bears responsibility for his brother's or sister's eternal welfare. That is what stewardship is all about; that is what Peter had in mind when he told us that we should be "good stewards of the manifold grace of God" (1Peter 4:10). James goes so far as to state that "pure religion and undefiled before God and the Father" is revealed by caring for "the fatherless and widows in their affliction" (James 1:27). Not that this defines the total significance of true religion, but that such service is an essential expression of genuine Christian concern for the needy. It is akin to the older bidding: "Thou shalt love thy neighbour as thyself" (Lev. 19:18; Matt. 22:39).

In company with the lawyer who led Jesus to state the second commandment, we might ask, "And who is my neighbour?" and might again study the answer that is wrapped in the parable of the good Samaritan (Luke 10:30-37). Jesus asked the questioner, "Which . . . was neighbour unto him that fell among the thieves?" and received the correct reply: "He that shewed mercy on him" (verses 36, 37). It was not the injured man who was the neighbor, except by implication; it was the Samaritan, who helped the helpless. Is not Christ thereby urging us to be good neighbors to those in need who come within reach of our compassion? And is not such Christian kindness to be the very essence of our religion?

Blessings on Stewardship

The Scriptures and experience teach us that faithfulness in stewardship does bring reward. When Israel was faithful in its duties toward God and its neighbors, the Lord's promises were generously fulfilled (Deut. 28:1-10; 2 Sam. 7:23, 24). When it slipped back into indifference and idolatry, the Lord repeatedly sent His servants the prophets, "daily rising up early and sending them: yet they hearkened not unto me, nor inclined their ear, but hardened their neck: they did worse than their fathers" (Jer. 7:25, 26). The last known of the many messengers was Malachi, probably contemporary with Nehemiah. He pleaded with both priests and people to resume the faithful practice of their religion, to support the Temple services, and to recapture their privileged relationship with their God. Their unchanging Lord was awaiting their return with arms that were full of blessings. "Prove me now herewith, saith the Lord of hosts, if I will not open you the windows of heaven, and pour you out a blessing, that there shall not be room enough to receive it. . . . And all nations shall call you blessed: for ye shall be a delightsome land" (Mal. 3:10-12). What a prospect! For the Jews, it ended in A.D. 70. For us it has a lively present and future.

The God whom we serve is neither subject to bribery nor does He engage in bribery. Neither is He mean or unresponsive to His people when they try to emulate His generosity and compassion toward His other children. "Blessed are the merciful," He assures us, "for they shall obtain mercy" (Matt. 5:7). And He does not offer pie in the sky by and by. In addition to the breathtaking realities of the new earth, more immediate blessings are promised to those who unselfishly serve as His stewards toward the unfortunate. "Give, and gifts will be given you. Good measure, pressed down, shaken together, and running over, will be poured into your lap." And with the promise there comes this principle: "Whatever measure you deal out to others will be dealt to you in return" (Luke 6:38, N.E.B.).

"Every kind and sympathizing word spoken to the sorrowful, every act to relieve the oppressed, and every gift to supply the necessities of our fellow beings, given or done with an eye to God's glory, will result in blessings to the giver. Those who are thus working are obeying a law of heaven and will receive the approval of God."—*Testimonies,* vol. 4, p. 56.

WE
BELIEVE
IN

THE CHURCH

We go to church on Sabbath. We support the church with our gifts. We are members of the Seventh-day Adventist Church in general and belong to a local church in particular. We may be vaguely aware that beyond those confines lies a shadowy body, approved by God but so large that it eludes our comprehension.

If we have such thoughts we should be encouraged, for we are on the right track. There are several meanings to the word *church*. A church can be a building, an organized local body of believers, an association of such bodies in a conference or union, or the General Conference of Seventh-day Adventists, which embraces all in the world who profess that faith. Even then there remains a larger body that must include sincere Christians who believe in and confess and serve the Lord Jesus Christ, while beyond all those there is a still wider circle embracing all God's sinless creatures who have been adoring Him from times eternal. The day will come when "every creature which is in heaven, and on the earth, and under the earth, and such as are in the sea, and all that are in them" shall join in ascribing "blessing, and honour, and glory, and power, . . . unto him that sitteth upon the throne, and unto the Lamb for ever and ever" (Rev. 5:13). Then, and not until then, "the great church victorious, Shall be the church at rest."

And we, in the meantime, shall refresh our

memories concerning the church on earth. In the beginning, when God created the heaven and earth, He must have intended the church to develop out of Eden, with every member of the human family becoming part of the immortal throng that no man can number. Sin ruined that plan and led to a more protracted fulfillment of the Creator's purpose, with some of His creatures choosing loyalty to Him while others chose His adversary. In the centuries that followed the Fall, the fortunes of the church appeared to rise and ebb as men and women embraced or rejected the salvation that was lovingly offered them. The far-sighted, however, have always known that the Almighty is working out His original purpose and will bring it to pass. In the Bible we can trace the stages by which that purpose will be fulfilled.

In the Old Testament

We should ever bear in mind that the records from Genesis to Malachi cover four thousand years and be prepared to meet the church in many different guises. At no time in that considerable span was her progress smooth: there were slow climbs and quick descents, a pattern that may be instructive for us today.

Because of the downward drag of sin the initiative in the formation of the church had to rest with God. No compulsion was needed, for He could always truthfully say to each potential church member, "I have loved thee with an everlasting love: therefore with lovingkindness have I drawn thee" (Jer. 31:3). In every age the pull of that love has been felt by choice and courageous spirits who have realized that "the things which are not seen are eternal," and who have "endured, as seeing him who is invisible" (2 Cor. 4:18; Heb. 11:27). Enoch was an early member of that select band, and it is possible that many of the other patriarchs had their eyes on heaven rather than on earth. Of Noah and his family there can be no doubt, in spite of their human weaknesses. With Abraham the pattern of "called out ones" is clearly set; the Lord had said to him, "Get thee out of thy country . . . : and I will make of thee a great nation, . . . and in thee shall all families of the earth be blessed" (Gen. 12:1-3). There was the nucleus of the church—a family growing into a nation (the Hebrews) through which all the earth would be blessed.

The vision of an elect people through whom the world would be brought back to God grew faint through Egyptian bondage and the ups and downs of the Exodus, but it was never completely lost. At the foot of Sinai and prior to Israel's entry into Canaan Moses conveyed to his people the challenging news from the Lord: "Ye shall be a peculiar treasure unto me above all people" (Ex. 19:5) and "Thou art an holy people unto the Lord thy God: the Lord thy God hath chosen thee to be a special people unto himself" (Deut. 7:6). In retrospect the New Testament saw the Hebrew congregation as the forerunner of the church, though Stephen's reference is to the "congregation in the wilderness" (Acts 7:38, margin) rather than to "the church."

But Israel did not meet the specifications, and it was on an individual rather than a national basis that any of its people became members of the 'êdâh or qâhâl, the assembly or congregation which was the forerunner of the church. Nevertheless, the vision was not entirely lost. Joshua and a few of the judges tried to preserve the ideal of a chosen people, Samuel endeavored to prolong the theocracy, and later prophets in the divided kingdom of Judah and Israel sought to inspire their compatriots to be loyal children of the Most High. Their successes were few; their disappointments were many.

In the Master's Ministry

When we move into the New Testament, we find ourselves in the presence of Him who does not see history through a glass darkly but knows the end from the beginning. He who had created the first church members, who appeared to Abraham (Gen. 18), to Jacob (Gen. 32:24-30), Moses (Ex. 3:1-6, 14; 34:5-9), and the nation Israel (1 Cor. 10. 4), who was dimly seen by psalmists and prophets (Ps. 110:1; Isa. 9:6, 7; 53; Jer. 23:5, 6; Dan. 9:24-27; Micah 5:2), and became flesh to dwell among men—He has an agelong knowledge of the church, and He knew the steps it would need to take for maturity.

When He who would reveal Himself as Lord of the church came to our world, one of His principal objectives was the founding of that body visible. To that end He chose and ordained, or appointed, twelve that they might be with Him, to learn of Him and from Him, "and that he might send them forth to preach" (Mark 3:13, 14). They grew under that experience, and the day came when He could unveil before their privileged eyes His vision of the church. He did this near the coastal town of Caesarea Philippi, where Peter declared, "Thou art the Christ, the Son of the living God." In response, Jesus promised, "Upon this rock I will build my church. . . . And I will give unto thee the keys of the kingdom of heaven: and whatsoever thou shalt bind on earth shall be bound in heaven: and whatsoever thou shalt loose on earth shall be loosed in heaven" (Matt. 16:13-19). Whatever might be our interpretation of this much-discussed passage, it does, beyond controversy, announce the formation of the church on the foundation of Christ's divinity. It lightly but firmly sketches the powers of the church, bearing in mind the disciples' limited understanding of its nature.

A year later the Lord was giving His soon-to-be apostles a wider view of the church's mission. The gospel of the kingdom would "be preached in all the world for a witness unto all nations" (chap. 24:14), and it was to be the eleven and their associates who were to do the preaching (Mark 16:14, 15). They were not unprepared: on the resurrection Sunday evening the Risen One had solemnly commissioned them: "As my Father hath sent me, even so send I you. And when he had said this, he breathed on them, and saith unto them, Receive ye the Holy Ghost" (John 20:21, 22). Fifty days afterward the final promise (Acts 1:8) was fulfilled, and the Christian church was on its way.

The Apostolic Church

Contrary to men's usual practice and to some ancient tradition, Jesus appointed no human successor to fill the void created by His own departure. In the forty days between His resurrection and ascension He made no effort to replace Judas; He left that task to the eleven and the remainder of the 120, who cared for it prayerfully and unanimously in the appointment of Matthias. The unanimity continued. "They were all with one accord in one place" (chap. 2:1). There they met the One of whom their Lord had spoken so much in the weeks before a cloud received Him out of their sight. The Holy Spirit came to them as promised, and they immediately recognized Him as Christ's successor.

This rich installment of church history must never be neglected, for it explains the unique, unhuman nature of the unity that prevailed in the early apostolic church. "They were all filled with the Holy Ghost" (verse 4). We may find it hard to define that experience, but at the least it meant that they allowed the Spirit to inspire their thoughts, their words, their deeds, their plans. This did not rob any of them of his personality but did bring all under one Guide. When domestic pressures raised difficulties between Hebrew and Hellenistic believers, "seven men of honest report, full of the Holy Ghost and wisdom" were appointed to care for the situation (chap. 6:1-8). When growth brought Jewish and Gentile Christians into disagreement over the need for circumcision and other ceremonial requirements (chap. 15:1-5), the Spirit led the first church council into an acceptable and workable compromise (verses 6-29). As growth continued, it was under the Spirit's impetus and guidance; His was the power and the wisdom that led the church through its first formative decades. But as death removed each of the apostles much of the first love was lost, the Spirit's leadership was sought less fervently, and His ministry played a less decisive role in church history. Human nature may have made this retrogression inevitable, but it was nonetheless regrettable.

Christ and His Church

No matter what the spiritual state of the church, Christ remains its Head. This is not subject to change; it is part of the Godhead's eternal intention for us and the universe. Paul saw this very clearly and built it into his understanding of universal history, sharing that view with us in his Epistles.

In his letter to the Colossians the apostle affirms the creatorship of Christ, His preexistence, His role in sustaining all that He made (Col. 1:16, 17). In verse 18 he introduces an additional concept, based on the human body, naming Christ as the Head and the church as the body. The context implies that the relationship is eternal, for Christ as Creator "is before all things." This establishes the eternity of the church in the divine program. It was not an idea that developed after the creation of our world but was there in the eternal mind prior to Creation. That causes no surprise to the Bible student; he remembers that Omniscience sees every stage of Creation—terrestrial and otherwise—before any creative act is undertaken. The church, we can conclude, has always been in our Lord's thinking.

We, however, are subject to strict temporal limitations and must therefore formulate our perceptions within a framework of time. The Creator, who made us that way, understands our restrictions and places His induction as Head of the church at the time of His resurrection, when God the Father "raised him from the dead, and set him at his own right hand..., and gave [or, appointed] him to be the head over all things to the church, which is his body" (Eph. 1:20-23).

A more exalted understanding of the close relation of the church to her Lord is impossible for us to grasp, though we must be careful not to push even the scriptural analogy too far. In creaturely life a head cannot function without a body, neither the body without the head. The two are parts of one whole. It is this unity that Paul teaches, with special stress on the dependence of the body upon the head—of the church upon Christ.

An extension of the physical illustration is drawn by Paul in Ephesians 5:22-32. The husband-wife relationship is seen as a symbol of the union between Christ and His church, with the husband representing Christ and the wife the church. As in an ideal marriage the husband is head of the wife, exercising a love-directed leadership, so Christ is the loving Head of the church. His love led Him to give Himself for the welfare of the church. He wanted to sanctify and cleanse it, that it might be "a glorious church," having no spot or wrinkle of any kind, being a holy church (verses 25-27). There we meet the Bridegroom and the bride, with the latter being totally dependent on her Husband for every beauty, virtue, and grace. This is surely the vision glorious for the church—to be the bride, the Lamb's wife, all glorious within and without, fit to reign with her Lord for ever and ever! How shall we relate that beatific concept to the group with whom we worship and the body to which we have chosen to belong—and how do they, in turn, relate it to us?

The Biblical concept of the church is so rich that

writers in both Testaments express it in several pictorial ways in addition to that of the head and body. One of the most appropriate is surely that which likens it to a temple or sanctuary, a building constructed specially for worship (chap. 2:19-22). In 1 Corinthians 6:19 and 2 Corinthians 6:16 the individual believer is described as "the temple of the Holy Ghost" and "the temple of the living God" on the grounds that God dwells in him (cf. 1 Cor. 3:16, 17). But the Ephesian concept is wider: it includes all saints, the apostles and prophets, the complete redeemed human family among whom God delights to live. The immediate application is of God in the Person of the Spirit living in the believing heart, but the longer view is of the Godhead's living among all the faithful who together form a living sanctuary where He is continually worshiped. How appropriate, how humbling, how inspiring, that the Most High, who "dwelleth not in temples made with hands," should make His living church His living temple!

When the New Testament was being written, formal church buildings did not exist. Congregations met in private homes or in the open air. Churches as we now know them were not constructed until Christianity became a recognized religion. It is ironic that many of the magnificent cathedrals were built in times of low-quality faith, while deep spirituality flourished in the plainest of buildings or when worshipers did not even have a roof over their heads. Maybe we need to learn the secret of beauty of building with beauty of character. The most dazzling picture in all Scripture is undoubtedly that of the New Jerusalem, "the holy city . . . coming down from God out of heaven, prepared as a bride adorned for her husband" (Rev. 21:2, 10-27). Significantly, the record of its descent is followed immediately by reference to God and the people among whom He will dwell (verse 3)). While the presence of God and the Son are the city's chief glory, the inhabitants, "the nations of them which are saved" (verse 24), are undoubtedly the most precious of all its splendors in the sight of the Father and Son. As a beloved bride is the most lovely of all sights in an adoring husband's eyes, so must the church "the bride, the Lamb's wife," arrayed in "the fine linen," which "is the righteousness of saints" (chap. 19:8), safely home in the Eternal City, appear to Him who has always loved her and has given Himself for her. Can the church do less now than to prepare for Him who is to be her Husband?

The Remnant Chuch

While we are naturally preoccupied with our own salvation—though happy are the saints who are so concerned with the redemption of others that they forget their own—it is a sobering fact that the membership of the church, the multitude which no man can number, is already largely settled, being composed of those who have died in the Lord from Adam and Eve onward. There now remain only those who will come safely through the last days.

These last ones are by no means forgotten. They receive special mention in Scripture, being described as "the remnant of her [the church's] seed, which keep the commandments of God, and have the testimony of Jesus Christ" (chap. 12:17). In John's later vision (chapter 14), they again receive notice. They are the fruitage of the preaching of the three angels' messages (verses 6-11), for "here are they," says the Revelator—the patient saints, the God-fearing commandment keepers who guard the faith of Jesus, or retain their faith in Jesus (verse 12). We who are alive today, the "last day," need to ensure that we are faithful members of that remnant and part of "the church of the firstborn, which are written in heaven" (Heb. 12:22, 23).

Those whom the Righteous Judge can justly include

in His church play a notable role in His eternal purpose—they demonstrate and thus make known "the wisdom of God in all its varied forms . . . to the rulers and authorities in the realms of heaven" (Eph. 3:10, N.E.B.). This is "the eternal purpose which he purposed in Christ Jesus our Lord" (verse 11). To us is given the honor of contributing to the fulfillment of that high purpose through faithful and fruit-producing membership in His church.

> "I love Thy Church, O God;
>   Her walls before Thee stand;
> Dear as the apple of Thine eye,
>   And graven on Thy hand.
>
> "For her my tears shall fall,
>   For her my prayers ascend,
> To her my cares and toils be given,
>   Till toils and cares shall end."
>
> —Timothy Dwight

WE
BELIEVE
IN

SYMBOLS FOR SAINTS

The distance from earth to heaven is great, immeasurable in miles or kilometers. Yet heaven can be nearer to us than any earthly object can ever be. Faith can span the distance and bring God the Spirit into the deepest recesses of our hearts and there create a little interim heaven that will link us to the larger heaven that is our Father's house.

But we need more than a connection with heaven; we need a preparation for heaven, be it the one that is "above the bright blue sky" or that later one that will be centered on earth. The Lord God knows that need and has provided two symbolic services that will both remind us of our eternal destination and bring us the grace to make the long journey. They both signify much more than the fulfillment of our simple illustration, but for the moment that purpose will suffice.

Symbols are helpful for our unspiritual natures; they give us a visible act or a tangible participation in outward ceremonies that help us to grasp unseen spiritual realities. These purposes are generously fulfilled in the Christian sacraments of baptism and the Lord's Supper. Neither is just what it appears to be; each means more, infinitely more, than its visible enactment suggests. Both are most precious to believers and the church because both have been blessed by our Lord, with the second having been instituted by Him and centering on Him.

Participation in the sacraments is efficacious only when faith operates and motivates the participant. Without faith the sacrament remains a mere form; with faith it becomes a life-bringing act. Here, more than anywhere else, we must recognize that "without faith it is impossible to please him: for he that cometh to God must believe that he is, and that he is a rewarder of them that diligently seek him" (Heb. 11:6). Let us, then, bring faith to bear on our study of the sacraments and on our participation in them.

Patterns

In the knowledge and providence of God it was through the Hebrew people that He conveyed His redeeming love to fallen mankind. The Hebrews were a practical people, their language was concrete rather than abstract, and they were given to illustrations from everyday life rather than remoter realms of philosophical thought. We can see this in the best-known psalm, with its pictures of the shepherd, green pastures, still waters, and the house of the Lord. Even Jesus reflected His human environment and taught in realistic parables and not through philosophy. It was left to Paul who, though a Hebrew, often reasoned as a Greek, to convey truth by means of less material images. Fortunately God is able to communicate in both types of language.

Such observations are applicable to the subject of patterns by which our God conveys to us eternal truths. Deliverance from sin was enacted through the Passover ceremonies. There was the house, the family, the father as priest, the lamb, the hyssop, the sprinkled blood, and the angel who passed over the homes of the Hebrews. Through that vivid enactment the Israelites found deliverance from Egypt and caught a glimpse of the science of salvation. We, from our vantage point in history, can learn even more from the midnight drama; we can see that "Christ our passover is sacrificed for us"

(1 Cor. 5:7). Then, like those Israelites, we must apply the benefits of the sacrifice to our own households so that each member of the family shares in the atonement and is saved from his sin and its penalty.

Further patterns emerged from the Exodus. The solution to each crisis was seen as a type for the Christian's journey through this life to the Promised Land. The first-century mind was less literalistic than ours and more ready to draw lessons that would seem somewhat far-fetched to the more materialistic thought of later generations. In the miraculous crossing of the Red Sea they saw an illustration of baptism, even though the point of the experience was that Israel "went into the midst of the sea upon the dry ground" (Ex. 14:22). Paul and his readers could see them "all baptized unto Moses in the cloud and in the sea" (1 Cor. 10:2), and he related that to the Christian's immersion in baptismal waters. From the provision of manna and the gift of water from the rock (Ex. 16:15; Num. 20:7-11), they saw the living bread and living water that were promised by Christ (John 6:31-35; 4:13, 14; 7:37, 38). It was then but a short step to use the supernaturally provided manna and water as symbols of the food and drink offered by Christ in the communion service.

Recognition of the ways in which the Bible interprets historical events can help to widen and deepen our understanding of the two sacraments that will now be studied in greater detail.

The Practice of Baptism

Baptism probably did not originate with John the Baptist, for Gentiles who wished to be recognized as Jews underwent proselyte baptism by immersion. John's audiences would therefore have little difficulty in understanding his call to "the baptism of repentance for the remission of sins" (Mark 1:4). They would even realize that it called for a complete change in life style, with confession of sin and restitution for wrongs committed (Luke 3:10-14).

But it was Christ's own submission to baptism and the divine acknowledgment of His self-dedication as the Holy Spirit descended upon Him in the form of a dove that gave significance to the rite. The Master's own explanation of His readiness to be baptized, even though He had no sin that called for repentance, was to set the standard for all who wished to follow His example: "Thus it becometh us to fulfil all righteousness." Who could decline baptism as a needless ceremony after this declaration from the Perfect One?

While there is no specific record of the disciples' having been baptized, the fact that Andrew and John were the Baptist's own followers and that it was Christ's own disciples who administered the rite during His ministry make it unthinkable that they themselves were not baptized. But be that as it may, the Lord's parting words commissioned them to "teach all nations, baptizing them" in the threefold name (Matt. 28:19). The day of Pentecost saw them promptly fulfilling the command. "And the same day there were added [to the church] . . . about three thousand souls" (Acts 2:41).

After that festal day, baptisms continued. There were baptisms of individuals such as the Ethiopian, Saul (chaps. 8:38; 9:18), and such families and households as those of Cornelius, the Philippian jailer, Crispus the Corinthian, and of believers at Ephesus (chaps. 10::48; 16:33; 18:8; 19:5), while in the town of Samaria its citizens and Simon Magus believed the preaching of Philip the deacon and were baptized (chap. 8:12, 13). Throughout the succeeding centuries the sacred rite of baptism has continued to serve as the door into the Christian church. Unfortunately, the unscriptural practice of infant baptism has robbed untold millions of the intended blessing that comes from adult baptism by immersion. The sacrament can be fully significant only when it is celebrated for those who have reached the age of accountability.

While there is mystery in the Christian religion, there is no room for magic of the abracadabra kind. It resists reduction to the mechanical; it insists on remaining superlatively spiritual. Its initial rite of baptism employs water for its enactment, but that water holds no supernatural quality—it is only a vehicle through which the candidate represents his cleansing and, deeper still, his death and subsequent resurrection.

But if the water remains the natural physical element that plays so important a part in our daily lives, in baptism it is partnered by the most spiritual of all spiritual possibilities—the Holy Spirit. "Except a man be born of water and of the Spirit," said Jesus to Nicodemus, "he cannot enter into the kingdom of God" (John 3:5). He might be immersed in water every day of his life, but unless he is born of the Spirit he will not be one step nearer the kingdom. On the other hand, it is possible to conceive of a man's being converted in the middle of a desert where no water was available for baptism. The significance of baptism, therefore, resides in the work done by the Spirit in the candidate's heart, which leads him to confess the death of his old self and the birth of the new by the symbolic act of momentary burial in, and subsequent emergence from, the baptismal water.

The theme of death and resurrection is explicitly taught by Paul as he reviews his own experience and that of his fellow Christians. "Know ye not," says he, "that so many of us as were baptized into Jesus Christ were baptized into his death?" (Rom. 6:3). That adds further precious meaning to the ordinance, not only signifying the death of the old life but sharing in the death of our Saviour, so that the repentant sinner can say, on being baptized, "I am crucified with Christ" (Gal. 2:20). After death comes burial, but not for long, for in the symbolization of baptism the Christian rises to walk in newness of life (Rom. 6:4). That can take place only if the old character has really died; otherwise it has only been in a coma, as it were, and will revert to sinful ways after baptism.

But whatever the true state of the one being baptized, the significance of the sacrament depends on the reality of divine intervention. Unless the Father raises us from death to new life, as He did with Jesus, we remain as spiritually dead as we were before baptism, and the rite has profited us nothing. Indeed, we might be worse for the experience, with hearts that have been hardened by the mockery of an ineffective symbolism and a haunting disappointment that could easily slide into disillusionment. Prevention of that sorry condition lies in sincerity, complete identification with and commitment to Christ, and continued renewal of the dedication intended in the solemnity of baptism.

The Last Supper

There is an impressive unity and continuity in sacred history, which is illustrated in the relation between the institution of the Passover in Egypt and that of the Last Supper in Jerusalem. As many as fourteen hundred years may have passed since the Israelites had celebrated their impending deliverance from Egyptian slavery (c. 1445 B.C.), and faithful members of the chosen race kept the observance alive under favorable and adverse circumstances.

When Jesus entered His twelfth year, He observed His first Passover with His parents in Jerusalem and there witnessed the service that He Himself had instituted for Israel in Egypt and that symbolized the sacrifice He would make for all people. As He grew older He saw more clearly the meaning of the annual celebration until, on the eve of the crucifixion, He was ready to make the Passover obsolete by the reality of His own vicarious death and triumph over the oppressor of God's people. At this crossroads of both sacred and human history He shared with His disciples the service that solemnized the end of the old and the beginning of the new understanding of redemption. His last supper with His companions would be their first Lord's Supper and a revelation of the true meaning of Passover ritual.

But the Saviour made no abrupt break with tradition. It would seem that He allowed the Passover meal to merge into the supper that first foreshadowed His death and victory and would soon commemorate those central events. He used the bread and wine that were part of the traditional meal and found them completely appropriate to His need, which was not surprising since they had been chosen in the first place as emblems of the sacrifice planned "before the foundation of the world."

With what deep unfathomable emotion must He have formed the words over the broken bread, "Take, eat: this is my body"; and over the wine, "This cup is the new testament in my blood." Those were some of the most solemn words ever to be uttered. If what some scientists tell us is true, they are still echoing around the circle of our earth. The day may come when we shall be able to recall them and learn from our Lord's own lips the full significance of each phrase. The disciples had to see their Master crucified, resurrected, and ascended before their meaning dawned upon them.

The Lord's Supper

While we humans are creatures of custom, repetition easily dulls the edge of our finest experiences. We therefore need to take deliberate steps to safeguard the most exalted experience of all, this side of eternity, as we share with fellow Christians the symbols of the death that effected our redemption. One proved way of guarding our appreciation for the communion service is to make each celebration the occasion for meditation upon the closing scenes of our Lord's earthly life, to spend that recommended thoughtful hour in contemplation of His words and acts in the upper room (*The Desire of Ages*, p. 83).

The Master provided us with the most effective preparation when He washed His disciples' feet and said, "I have given you an example, that ye should do as I have done to you"(John 13:15). Unless we side with Judas, our hearts will soften at the thought of our Saviour's loving humility, and we shall find our spirits in harmony with His.

> "Drop, drop, slow tears,
>   And bathe those beauteous feet
> Which brought from Heaven
>   The news and Prince of Peace:
>
> * * * * *
>
> "In your deep floods
>   Drown all my faults and fears;
> Nor let His eye
>   See sin, but through my tears."
>   —Phineas Fletcher

Jesus well knew how easily forgetfulness comes to the human heart. He therefore gave the sacramental service to refresh our minds, to keep memory bright with a clear vision of the supper table where He said, "This do in remembrance of me" (Luke 22:19). Participation in that service does more than remind; it enables us to share the disciples' experience, to sit with Christ, to eat the bread and drink the wine He offers as symbols of His atoning sacrifice, to review the price He paid to save us from our sins, and to respond by forsaking those sins and pledging renewed allegiance to Him who loved us and gave Himself for us.

The deliberate, conscious effort to recall the solemn significance of that evening communion will not go unrewarded. It will help us to re-create the simple beauty of that memorable night, enabling us to join the apostles in their remembrance and to accept from the Lord's hands the bread and wine that will cleanse and invigorate us for living the Christ life here below.

In Memoriam

It is providential that Biblical instruction on the communion service is not limited to the four Gospels but is continued and enriched by Paul's teaching in his first Epistle to the Corinthians. Earlier references to "breaking of bread" in the book of Acts (chaps. 2:42, 46; 20:7, 11) are somewhat ambiguous and may not record celebration of the sacrament. But in 1 Corinthians 10, while discussing the believers' attitude to food offered to idols, he reveals that Communion was being celebrated in the Christian church about twenty-six years after Christ's ascension (verses 16-21). In chapter 11 he passes from an incidental mention and records his own understanding of the sacred meal as "received of the Lord" (verse 23). His account harmonizes with those of the evangelists while contributing additional features that are precious to the Christian community.

Paul employs similar language to Luke's when he records Christ's words, "This do in remembrance of me" (Luke 22:19; 1 Cor. 11:24, 25), and in so doing emphasizes the memorial nature of the service. It was instituted to remind the apostles and their converts of their Lord and His redemptive acts. Its purpose is defeated if it does not vividly recall those scenes to mind.

There is a concluding purpose that should be served by the act of Communion. Jesus disclosed it when, just prior to the singing of the Passover hymn, He spoke of drinking "this fruit of the vine" with the disciples in His Father's kingdom (Matt. 26:29). There is no element of doubt here; He expects to be there to welcome them.

Paul expresses the same confidence by saying, "As often as ye eat this bread, and drink this cup, ye do shew the Lord's death till he come" (1 Cor. 11:26). Of Christ's death there could be no doubt; these words show the same certainty about His return. The sacrament thus looks both backward and forward—back to the crucifixion weekend and forward to the triumphant Second Advent, when Master and disciples will be reunited in their Father's kingdom.

That anticipated Advent certainly encourages us to be faithful communicants at the Lord's table now, that we might there find mercy and grace to be ready for our Saviour's appearing, and fitness for life in His Father's eternal kingdom.

WE
BELIEVE
IN

CHRISTIAN WITNESS

If God chose, he could so unveil His majesty that every living creature in heaven and earth would be compelled by the seeing of his eyes and the hearing of his ears and the dictate of his heart to confess that the Father is Lord God Almighty.

That day will come. It is written, "As I live, saith the Lord, every knee shall bow to me, and every tongue shall confess to God" (Rom. 14:11, cf. Isa. 45:23). But that day is not yet, for the Almighty seeks those who will worship Him from the compulsion of love and not from the fear of might. When they have been found and brought into His kingdom, then will come the removal of the veil and the revelation of His might that will bring the universe to its knees, confessing, "Great and marvellous are thy works, Lord God Almighty; just and true are thy ways, thou King of saints" (Rev. 15:3).

In the meantime God, in His infallible wisdom, chooses to place His publicity in the hands and the lives of those whose eyes have been opened by His love to see His nature and His power and who are equipped and willing to declare their discoveries to their fellows. "You yourselves are my witnesses—it is Yahweh who speaks—my servants whom I have chosen, that men may know and believe me and understand that it is I" (Isa. 43:10, Jerusalem). That appointment embraced Israel in Isaiah's day and the church in ours. It shows how the Lord depends on His chosen people to be His representatives, those that represent Him and His policies to an estranged world.

The character of God is so misunderstood and the misunderstanding drives so many multitudes away from Him that the need for reliable witnesses to His unchanging goodness increases as we get nearer to the close of human history. Those witnesses must be drawn from the ranks of those who have tasted and seen that the Lord is good (Ps. 34:8; 1 Peter 2:3) and can testify from personal experience that "blessed are all they that put their trust in him" (Ps. 2:12). In such work an ounce of practice is worth a ton of theory!

Essential Qualification

It is remarkable that He to whom all power was given in heaven and in earth should feel the need at the very outset of His ministry for human assistants. It would not have been beyond God's devising to have evangelized our world without human aid, but He then would have saved a host of flabby-muscled Christians who would have been unaware of the cost and the rewards of bringing a soul into the kingdom of heaven. That would be a frustrating operation. One of the Son's earliest tasks, then, was the recruitment of twelve who would continue His work when He returned to the glory from which He had come. Those twelve He trained, "that they should be with him, and that he might send them forth to preach" (Mark 3:14).

The duties attached to that appointment were demanding, but the recompense was to be proportionately great. "Whosoever therefore shall confess me before men, him will I confess also before my Father which is in heaven" (Matt. 10:32). The phrase "confess me" literally reads "confess in me" in the original and conveys the thought of being "in Christ" and publicly acknowledging that oneness, that unity, comes with being identified with Him so that all know to whom one belongs. Whosoever makes such a bold, consistent, fruitful confession will, in turn, be fully acknowledged by Christ in His Father's presence.

The disciples ran up a good score in this matter of "confession," or witness, as they accompanied their Leader on His preaching and healing missions throughout Palestine, but after He had left them, His training yielded still greater fruitage. Following His instructions, they tarried in Jerusalem until they were "endued with power from on high." Then they became witnesses concerning all the amazing events that had transpired before them, first in Jerusalem, then in all Judea, and in Samaria, and eventually to the utmost bounds of the then-known world (Luke 24:48, 49; Acts 1:8; 2:32). That was confession, or witness, of the most effective order.

It is clear from the contemporary records that there was nothing perfunctory about this apostolic witness. The witnesses were under compulsion, certainly, but not of a tyrannical kind. "We cannot but speak the things which we have seen and heard," declared Peter and John before the Jewish authorities (Acts 4:20). "We . . . were eyewitnesses of his majesty," wrote Peter to fellow Christians at a later date (2 Peter 1:16), while John writes of "that which was from the beginning, which we have heard, which we have seen with our eyes, which we have looked upon, and our hands have handled, . . . the Word of life" (1 John 1:1). That was dynamic witness. It accounted for much of the remarkable growth of the church in the first century. A late twentieth-century counterpart could yield similar results.

The First Witnesses

Countless sermons have been preached on the value of one-to-one witness, and such exhortations will continue, for they are needed, they are based on New Testament experience, and they are endorsed by the Lord Jesus.

The pattern, as traced by John, led to the call of the first disciples. John the Baptist drew the attention of two of his own followers to Jesus by saying, "Behold the Lamb of God!" (John 1:36). As a result of that direct testimony Andrew and John became the young Preacher's first disciples. Andrew was quick to learn and apply the lesson that had introduced him to Jesus. "He first findeth his own brother Simon, and saith unto him, We have found the Messias. . . . And he brought him to Jesus" (verses 41, 42). He captured the whole truth of his encounter within the confines of that one brief phrase, "We have found the Messias," which was the most startling news that one Jew could bring to another. He then used the news in the best possible way—he shared it with his nearest relative, his brother Simon. How the twentieth-century church would grow if that sequence always followed our face-to-face meetings with the Saviour!

Jesus took the next step in building His working fraternity—He "findeth Philip, and saith unto him, Follow me" (verse 43). That initiative placed an immediate responsibility on Philip's shoulder. He had been sought; he must do some seeking. He responded with alacrity, bearing a testimony similar to Andrew's as he had sought Simon. "Philip findeth Nathanael, and saith unto him, We have found him, of whom Moses in the law, and the prophets, did write," and when Nathanael came face to face with Jesus, he too recognized the divine nature and swiftly confessed, "Thou art the Son of God; thou art the King of Israel" (verses 45-49).

The technique worked. Personal introductions made by friend to friend brought the future apostles into the presence of their Lord and their God. Jesus Himself was a link in the chain of enlistment, as He ever will be, but that chain lengthened because those who had come within range of His dynamic, sanctifying personality were willing to share their newfound faith with relatives and friends.

The unnamed Samaritan woman found her inspiration in Christ's knowledge of her irregular marital status, which even today would have inhibited almost any thought of witness. But the loving skill of the Stranger's approach had captured her. She ignored the disciples' scorn, and she, who must have been notorious, witnessed so persuasively to her fellow Samaritans that they flocked to see Him who had made so deep an impression on her. So it may be, even today, even with those who seem farthest removed from our Lord's converting influence.

Witness to Miracles

The Gospels leave no doubt that Christ's miracles caused a great stir throughout Palestine and that this was sometimes contrary to the Lord's desire. He discouraged the easy publicity that accompanies the visibly miraculous—the healing of lepers, the restoration of sight, the feeding of thousands. There were two wonders, however, on which He placed no restrictions—that of the transformed life and His own resurrection from the grave.

A dramatic illustration of the first exception is set in the hills that lead down to the eastern shore of Gennesaret, or Lake Galilee. There Jesus met "a man with an unclean spirit," or as Matthew reports the incident, "two possessed with devils"—mad men or lunatics, they might be called today (Mark 5:1-20; Matt. 8:28-34). The Lord cured the demented creature who, to the wonder of all who knew him, sat peacefully, "clothed, and in his right mind" (Mark 5:15). The healed man, understandably enough, wanted to remain with his Deliverer; but Jesus had a better idea. "Go home to thy friends, and tell them how great things the Lord hath done for thee, and hath had compassion on thee" (verse 19). What harder assignment could one expect? And what more effective opportunity for certifying the miracle of restoration and testifying of Him who had brought about the transformation? The healed man's appearance before his neighbors could hardly have been less spectacular than that of Jonah's in the streets of Nineveh! His case was unanswerable. It was similar to the blind man's when he declared, "One thing I know, that, whereas I was blind, now I see" (John 9:25). The Gergesene scarcely needed to make that explanation, for all could see the drastic change that had taken place. His energies could concentrate on telling his friends how great things the Lord had done for him. What more persuasive evidence in favor of Christ could any man offer?

But from a Bible's-eye point of view—and beyond serious dispute—the greatest of all miracles is the resurrection of the crucified Christ from His tomb early on that long-ago Sunday morning. That unique event turned the fearful into heroes, sinners into saints, sent the church on its conquering way, and turned the world upside down. Even the pagan guards testified to the amazing occurrence, while Mary Magdalene, several other women, John, Peter, and the other disciples, Cleopas and his companion, and "above five hundred brethren at once" all joined in declaring that they had personally seen the Resurrected One after His burial. That vivid remembrance and their compulsion to share it with others provided much of the power that convinced thousands that Jesus is the Christ, the Son of God.

Secret of Witnessing

It will be readily agreed that it was not just the historical fact of the Resurrection that motivated the first Christians in their persistent efforts to convert the world to their way of thinking. They saw it as victory over the evil that condemned Him to die, as defeat for the enemies of righteousness, as evidence for His divinity, and as an earnest of the ultimate triumph of God's redemptive purposes. They also saw in it a convincing display of the Father's love for His Son and the people the Son had come to save, and of the power to support all the love that had been poured out through the Son's unselfish ministry.

But to those who were most deeply moved by the Godhead's concern, there was a further reaction: demonstrations of divine love drove them to nurture similar love in themselves toward their fellows. Paul goes so far as to say that Christ's "purpose in dying for all was that men, while still in life, should cease to live for themselves, and should live for him who for their sake died and was raised to life" (2 Cor. 5:15, N.E.B.). There lay the motive power in the missionary surge that seized those early Christians. In a form suited to our own personalities, environment, and experience, it needs to be the propelling power behind our service also. Without it we may be only dummies manipulated into service by promotional leaders.

How to Witness

From an idealistic point of view it is a pity that we ever need to pose the question, "How shall we witness?" Those who first heard the apostles' preaching cried, "Men and brethren, what shall we do?" (Acts 2:37), but that concerned the step that followed conviction, and Peter promptly answered, "Repent, and be baptized" (verse 38). And "they that gladly received his word were baptized" (verse 41), but they hardly seemed to have needed instruction about their subsequent Christian duty. They had all things in common, they sold their possessions and shared the proceeds with the needy. They praised God and found favor with all the people; "and the Lord added to the church daily such as should be saved" (verses 44-47). Their dedicated fervor impelled them to witness. They told what the Lord had done for them, their transparent sincerity carrying such conviction that their number increased by leaps and bounds.

In sharing their newfound faith in so spontaneous a manner, those converts were but following their Lord's counsel. From the beginning of His ministry He had counseled His followers in the most effective form of witness when He said, "Let your light so shine before men, that they may see your good works" (Matt. 5:16). There was to be nothing forced or artificial about their Christian service. The practical product of their religion, their "good works," was to be as evident as the light that effortlessly shines from a lamp and illumines all around. Even so would the radiance from genuine Christian conduct lead others to glorify their heavenly Father. "The unstudied, unconscious influence of a holy life is the most convincing sermon that can be given in favor of Christianity. Argument, even when unanswerable, may provoke opposition; but a godly example has a power that is impossible wholly to resist."—*The Acts of the Apostles*, p. 511.

But we must not run away with the idea that witness is to be wholly passive and unconscious, for the same Lord who advised us to let our light shine also commanded, "Go ye into all the world, and preach" (Mark 16:15). The light from our personal lamps is limited in its range. If the whole world is to be lightened with the gospel's glory, the individual lights need to be evenly spaced to ensure maximum coverage and must be greatly multiplied, or there must be a conscious effort to share the gospel blessings with "every creature." Even then the best results come when professional preaching comes from the lips of those whose lives completely harmonize with the message they proclaim. There is, then, no way that a Christian can escape responsibility for the quality of the life he leads.

Christ's teaching has an uncanny pervasiveness that

leaves no corner of our lives and no mite of our responsibilities untouched. His authority and His impulsion are omnipresent and inescapable. We might "take the wings of the morning, and dwell in the uttermost parts of the sea; [but] even there shall ... [his] hand lead" us, and His "right hand shall hold" us. This places on each of us a global responsibility for witness far and near, with no ready-made pardon for neglect of one or the other. As G. K. Chesterton would remind us:

> "The dreadful joy Thy Son has sent
> Is heavier than any care;
> We find, as Cain his punishment,
> Our pardon more than we can bear."

We may indeed find the weight of Christian duty to be much greater than we bargained for, but it must not therefore be jettisoned.

> "Lord, when we cry Thee far and near
> And thunder through all lands unknown
> The gospel into every ear,
> Lord, let us not forget our own."

Results of Witness

The results are assured. The God who made our world and gave His Son to save it from the havoc wrought by sin will not allow His purpose to be thwarted. He has given men their freedom of choice; He sends messengers to persuade them to return to Him, and He has promised those messengers, "My word ... shall not return unto me void, but it shall accomplish that which I please, and it shall prosper in the thing whereto I sent it" (Isa. 55:11).

The promise God gave to Paul when He made him a minister and a witness belongs also to all who accept a similar though smaller commission. "[I will deliver] thee from the people, and from the Gentiles," He told the newly converted Saul, and then He sketched the responsibilities that were being laid upon him. Implicit in each assignment was the assurance of success. The missionary was "to open their eyes, . . . to turn them from darkness to light, and from the power of Satan unto God," and he was to do this for the express purpose of bringing them "forgiveness of sins, and inheritance among them which are sanctified by faith that is in me" (Acts. 26:16-18). This is the Lord's way of accomplishing His beneficent purpose. It is His method of leading His prodigal children back to their Father's home.

In varying degrees, according to one's calling, talents, and opportunities, this is the office to which all Christians are called. Conversion is not meant to provide a magic carpet on which the neophyte is wafted painlessly and responsibility-free into the kingdom of heaven. "Every true disciple is born into the kingdom of God as a missionary."—*The Desire of Ages,* p. 195. Pastor Peter teaches this to the readers of his first Epistle (chap. 2:9-12) as he spreads before us the glories of our calling: "Ye are a chosen generation, a royal priesthood, an holy nation, a peculiar people," or "a people belonging to God" (Weymouth). At the same time, in equally clear language, he depicts our duties: We are to show forth the praises, or the virtues, of Him who has called us out of our unchristian darkness into His marvelous light. Fulfillment of this high calling demands that we "abstain from fleshly lusts, which war against the soul," and live such exemplary lives that even our most severe critics will see our good works and will be led to glorify God.

There we have the heart of the doctrine of Christian witness. Every faithful child of God can grasp it and by the grace of our Lord put it into practice in the circumstances in which God has placed him.

WE
BELIEVE
IN

THE LIFE THAT COUNTS

The life does count! We are continually being judged, especially with regard to our religion, by the quality of the life we live. And there is nothing unfair in such judgment, for religion that does not produce a winsome life, the quality of character that we most admire but despair of ever attaining—that brand of religion has failed in its principal objective.

The life that fails receives great publicity. "If that's your religion, I want nothing to do with it!" The life that succeeds may not be so widely advertised, but it is noted. "If all Christians were like her [or him], I might consider joining the church!"

From a practical angle, then, we might suggest that the question of the quality of our Christianity touches on the most important of all doctrines, that of being born again and growing up into spiritual maturity. This is the goal of our religion. If the goal is not reached, our acceptance of and adherence to other teachings have been little more than academic exercises that may have brightened or restricted our life on earth but will not have led us into the kingdom of heaven.

In varied ways the Holy Scriptures impress that lesson upon us. The Master taught it to Nicodemus, telling him of the paramount need to be born anew and to develop from spiritual babyhood to full maturity. Paul shows a similar concern with development, encouraging his converts to grow up into Christ, having

His moral stature as their goal (Eph. 4:13-15). The theme appealed strongly to Peter, and it is he who took up his Lord's teaching and wrote of "being born again . . . by the word of God" and of being "newborn babes," nourished on "the sincere milk of the word" and growing thereby. When he came to give his closing counsel to the faithful, it took the form of an exhortation to "grow in grace, and in the knowledge of our Lord and Saviour Jesus Christ" (2 Peter 3:18). What better advice could he leave to his original readers and to us? We should plan to keep on growing in spiritual grace and in a personal knowledge of our Saviour and to live lives that will bring Him glory both now and forever.

Our Inner Life

It was not merely poetic fancy that led prophets and poets to declare, "The Lord is my rock, and my fortress, and my deliverer; my God, my strength, in whom I will trust" (Ps. 18:2). Their confidence came from experience; they had learned to know the strength and reliability of the God whom they served. David could confidently say, "Though an host should encamp against me, my heart shall not fear" (Ps. 27:3). Through sunshine and shadow he had come to place full trust in the God of his salvation. This experiential knowledge he was willing and eager to share with others.

Isaiah knew the same God as the psalmist and possessed a confidence similar to David's. When viewing his people's needs, he reminded them that God will keep those in perfect peace whose minds are trustfully stayed on Him (Isa. 26:3). Just as a tired passenger can sleep peacefully in a car when he knows that a good driver is at the wheel, so can we be at rest, knowing that God has our world in His hands. That confidence we should be able to share with others, saying, "Trust ye in the Lord for ever: for in the Lord Jehovah is everlasting strength" (verse 4).

It is not necessary for our trust always to be cast in a heroic mold. Indeed, the greater need for most of us is for the more commonplace variety that will help us meet everyday needs and their small emergencies. They call for what has been so beautifully described as "the practice of the presence of God," which consists of cultivating the constant presence of our Lord so faithfully that He is with us and we with Him at every moment of the day and night, waking and sleeping. We are conscious of His companionship in work and play, in worship and in relaxation, and when night comes we can say, "I laid me down and slept; I awaked; for the Lord sustained me" (Ps. 3:5).

It is not natural to live with anyone day in and day out without holding conversation with that companion. With God that is called communion, and that is an essential part of the life that counts. The Christian needs to cultivate the habit of talking with his Lord at any hour of the day or night, for "they that wait upon the Lord shall renew their strength" (Isa. 40:31). The silent prayer, the heavenward thought, the devotional reading, the quiet hour of study when we consciously wait upon the Lord—these will sustain the inner life that is essential for holiness in our workaday world.

The Aspiring Life

If we do not aspire, we shall never see the kingdom of heaven; we shall remain earthbound and never rise higher than man can take us. Aspiration, then, is essential to salvation. We must want to reach for the stars, to "seek those things which are above, where Christ sitteth on the right hand of God" (Col. 3:1). But we must do more than seek; we must set our affections, or minds, on things above and take them off things that are on the earth (verse 2). That calls for mental and spiritual discipline, yet discipline alone will not suffice. We must be numbered among those who "hunger and thirst after righteousness," so ardently desiring to be right with God that we cannot be satisfied until we attain that blessed state.

In every age there have been choice spirits who have longed for union with their Maker. Some of the most ardent came to be known as saints; others were outwardly indistinguishable from their neighbors, yet their citizenship was in heaven. They repeated the psalmist's confession, saying, "My soul longeth, yea, even fainteth for the courts of the Lord: my heart and my flesh crieth out for the living God" (Ps. 84:2). To all such aspirants the title of "blessed" is given, "for they shall be filled," or satisfied (Matt. 5:6). "All who long to bear the likeness of the character of God shall be satisfied. The Holy Spirit never leaves unassisted the soul who is looking unto Jesus. He takes of the things of Christ and shows them unto him."—The Desire of Ages, p. 302.

Our Family Life

For the majority of earth's population the normal, natural place in which to eat meals is with the family in the home. If that were also true of spiritual food, our world would be a happier, more law-abiding planet. If one could establish just one beneficial custom for the good of our troubled society, the habit of daily family worship would be one of the most effective.

A home that failed to supply food for its occupants would soon be empty, either by the removal or death of its occupants. Yet there are thousands upon thousands of nominal Christian homes where spiritual food through family devotions is never supplied. Their members are expected to survive on one meal per week, taken in church, while they are allowed to starve for the other six days. Such cruel neglect is contrary to the divine will and the divine plan for mankind. "Give us this day our daily bread," Christ taught us to pray. Parents and children should join forces to ensure that the prayer is fulfilled.

In Christian homes family worship is relatively easy to begin but is not always easy to maintain. It calls for consistent leadership from parents and discipline for the children, but the end more than justifies any struggles that are necessary for firm adherence to the morning and evening program. How can we fulfill the Biblical injunction, "Bring them [the children] up in the nurture and admonition of the Lord" (Eph. 6:4), if we do not daily train them by prayer and study of the Scriptures? A home can receive no higher accolade than that which comes from those who praise the exemplary Christian lives of its children!

Our Social Life

Human nature clearly has not changed between Paul's day and our own. Today's "old man" is cast in a similar mold to the character with which the apostle had to deal. The portrait that he unconsciously paints of the church members at Colossae shows that they battled against the same sins that beset us today (Col. 3:5-9). There are the all too familiar forms of sexual immorality, which ring the death knell over true spirituality if they are not conquered, and greed, which squeezes the breath out of genuine religion. In addition are those failings that cause so much distress to others and for which the tongue is so often the instrument—anger and rage, malice, slander, filthy talk, and lies.

These sins, says the apostle, are those we should have left behind us at the time of baptism, when we were born again. The new nature, which should have then appeared, is able to overcome all our evil tendencies. Furthermore that nature will, if we permit, be continually renewed by its personal knowledge of Christ its Creator in whose likeness it has been formed (Col. 3:9, 10). This new life proclaims, more clearly than any other evidence, the genuineness of our religion.

In a multiracial church whose members are drawn from every nation, kindred, tongue, and people, there is one other area in which the born-again Christian spirit should burn very brightly. Christlike race relations should be easier for us than for the early Christians, when social barriers set forbidding distances between so many levels of society. But the same qualities are needed now as then, for the natural human heart harbors the same prejudices in the twentieth as in the first century. Furthermore, those virtues are needed by all people, no matter what their position on the artificial social scale (verse 11). The privileged, the rich, the educated, the powerful, need much of Christ's spirit in their relations with their less fortunate brothers and sisters. Just as surely, though in an inverse direction, similar grace is needed by other sections of society as they struggle to exercise Christian understanding toward those who have so much compared with their little. It may help if we remember the situations that confronted Jesus and His followers in Roman-occupied Palestine. What patience, forgiveness, and tolerance were demanded of them; what an example they can provide for us!

Our Quality of Life

As we recognize the demands that present social realities place upon us we more readily confess our need for spiritual gifts to fulfill those obligations and welcome the help afforded by our religion. That help was available to those first courageous souls in the eastern Mediterranean world who became Christians; the same help is available to us now. As "the elect of God, holy and beloved, " we too may put on compassion, kindness, humility, gentleness, and patience, lovingly remembering what Christ has done for us and recognizing what we may do for others (verses 12, 13). The total solution is still to be found in the greatest of all spiritual gifts, that of love. Genuine Christlike love is able to walk through social barriers and unite in one body those who would otherwise remain poles apart (verse 14).

Desirable though it may be, such a blessed state of unity does not come from a casual flood of good feeling or an occasional surge of brotherly love. We need a firmer base than that of passing emotions. We must, as Paul tells us (verses 15-17), let the peace that comes from Christ control our hearts in the interests of unity. Christ's word, contained in the Bible and given to us by His Holy Spirit, will give us the wisdom that is needed in the delicate area of human relations. Common acts of worship—teaching, counseling, praising God by singing psalms, hymns, and spiritual songs, expressing mutual thanks to the Father—these will bind into one body men, women, young people, and children of widely differing backgrounds and enable us to say:

> "In Christ now meet both east and west,
>   In Him meet south and north;
> All Christly souls are one in Him
>   Throughout the whole wide earth."
> —John Oxenham

So far as self is concerned—and that is usually a great concern—the goal of true religion is eternal life. That is not an entirely selfish concept, for he who is keen enough on life eternal to pursue it is usually intelligent enough to realize that it cannot be gained in an unsplendid isolation. That much he has learned from his Master.

After Peter's magnificent confession and his mistaken concern for his Lord's life, Jesus shared with His disciples a piece of other-worldly philosophy that was and still is at variance with human inclinations: "If any man will come after me, let him deny himself, and take up his cross, and follow me" (Matt. 16:24). The fact that we have read so far indicates our interest in following Christ, but who *wants* to deny himself, who *wants* to take up such a cruel load as a cross? Is there no other way to follow Him? Apparently not, for it is His way, the way He took to accomplish His purpose of taking away the sin of the world, and those who want to follow must tread in those self-sacrificing steps.

A Means to an End

But hold on. Denial and cross-carrying are not the end of the story; they are means to an end, that end being eternal life. He who balks at self-denial and makes the saving of his own life his chief end will lose that life—and that is tragedy. The brighter side of the picture, though seemingly still dark, shows that he who for Christ's sake has not selfishly clung to his own life and interest will find life, life eternal. A paradox? Certainly, but that is Christ's way, and it works. It has produced the greatest lives in human history, and the end is not yet. It can produce greatness and longevity in our lives too—life everlasting, life for eternity, which is what Jesus wants for each of us.

And now our prolonged study of some of Christianity's principal doctrines draws to its close. We have only touched on some of them, and that quite lightly. Some may meet a specific need in our own spiritual pilgrimage; others may at present seem less important, but they are nonetheless milestones on the road to a complete understanding of God's will for each of us. They all are given to guide us on our heavenward way. But we shall not reach the Holy City on the strength of our own energies. We need, as Jude foresaw (verses 24, 25), to commit ourselves and one another to Him who is able to keep us from falling and to bring us into His glorious presence without blemish and with great joy. That Person is the only wise God, who is our Saviour through the ministry of Jesus Christ our Lord; to Him be glory and majesty, dominion and power, as before time began, now and forevermore.

May each of these truths that we hold so triumph that all may play a part in leading us into the glorious presence of the Father, the Son, and the Holy Spirit. Amen.